MW00377362

Everybody Needs a Brain Tumor

As told by David Koelliker

Written by John Koelliker

Copyright © 2017 John Koelliker

All rights reserved.

ISBN-13: 978-0692993118
ISBN-10: 0692993118

To the woman of my dreams, my nurse, my rock, my best friend, my dear wife.

Contents

Preface

"Judge a man by his questions rather than his answers."

—Voltaire

The title of this book may lead you to open these pages because of a question. You may be thinking, "Why would anyone in their right mind make the claim that everybody needs a brain tumor? That person must not have a heart, much less a brain!" Well, if you had any thoughts similar to that, I don't blame you. If I were in your shoes, I'd probably be thinking the same thing.

But I've actually had another question on my mind. It's a question that's been rattling around in my head for the past eight years. I never asked, "Why me?" or "How could this happen to me?" but rather, "Now that

I've been diagnosed with a terminal brain tumor, how do I live now?" I can't say I've learned the answer to this question, and to be honest, I don't know if there is a clear answer to this question. However, the past eight years of fighting this brain tumor have brought me some clarity on this topic. I'd like to share those thoughts with you, but my hope is that as you read my story, your own answers will be unfolded.

Everybody Needs a Brain Tumor isn't a book only for those with brain tumors; it's not about death, and I certainly hope it's not a pity party. Rather, this book is about living in difficult and even terminal situations and still being happy. It's one man's story about his fight with a brain tumor, how it affected his life, and what it taught him. It's a book about opportunity. It's a book about life, love, and hope.

Many of you have picked up this book because you or someone you love dearly has recently been diagnosed with a brain tumor, or you've experienced another form of cancer, disease, or tragedy. According to the American Brain Tumor Association, 79,000 new cases of primary brain tumors are expected to be diagnosed in 2017. Roughly 32% are malignant. This means that every day, almost one hundred people are told not only that they have a brain tumor, but that their tumor is malignant and their life will most definitely be cut short. Many times, it means they have approximately three to eighteen months to live.

More than anything, my heartfelt desire is to give you a hug and tell you that I am deeply sorry. There is no disease, sickness, or situation that is identical to another, and I don't pretend to understand the challenges you are facing. Although my condolences are inadequate, I really do wish the best for you and those suffering alongside you.

As a young boy, I was taught that a foundational principle of our existence is the law of opposition. To know light, one must experience darkness. To know hot, one must experience cold. To know sweet, one must know bitter. Experiencing opposites helps us to appreciate and understand everything in life. However, there isn't a good way to experience the opposite of life, which is death. Without being able to experience death, we sometimes struggle to understand life. We live our lives worried about menial things and forget to appreciate what really matters.

This childhood lesson has stayed with me throughout my life, but it has only become real since my diagnosis. My brain tumor has taught me to consider death, and therefore understand life a little better. And therein lies the basis for the title of this book. Why does everybody need a brain tumor? Everybody needs a brain tumor because it teaches you how to live with the possibility of death. And only through considering what it is to die do we truly understand what it is to live.

DAVID KOELLIKER

Chapter 1

The Beginning

I remember the first time I went to the beach. As one of seven children, family vacations weren't easy for my parents, but we had finally driven the twelve hours from Salt Lake City, Utah, to Newport Beach, California. The beach always seemed like such a magical place to me, and I was thrilled to finally see it for myself. I was only seven years old, but I remember this vacation like it happened yesterday. When we arrived, I immediately fell in love with everything that beach life entailed—building sand castles, playing catch, and feeling the cold water roll over my feet.

Most of all, I loved racing the waves. I would run into the shallow water, wait for a wave to come, and then run as fast I could to escape the wave. I wasn't a great swimmer, so I didn't dare go too deep, but this was my way of playing in the ocean. My siblings and I would race the waves for hours on end.

On one of the last days of our vacation, the waves were much bigger and seemed to be breaking closer to the shore. I wasn't afraid, though. I had spent most of the week running away from waves, so I didn't feel like that day would be any different. After barely escaping the crash of a few waves, I got a little more daring and went out farther into the shallow water. As I watched the wave come closer, I immediately realized that I had mistimed its arrival. The wave was bigger than I had anticipated, and I was stuck in water that was too deep to escape before the wave hit. I started pushing through the current with my little legs, trying to run as fast as I could. Panic set in as I realized that I wasn't making any progress. I felt desperate, and my body went numb with fear.

Seconds later, the wave crashed down on me and sent me somersaulting toward the hard sand floor. The whirlwind of water and sand picked me up a couple of times and tossed me around like a rag doll. After a few seconds, the water calmed and retreated for the next wave. I scrambled to my feet, terrified, but okay. I sprinted to my parents as fast as I could with tears and scratches covering my face. The force of that wave scared me so badly that I didn't go near the ocean for the rest of the trip.

Thirty-three years later, my wife and I took our five children to Newport Beach for a family vacation. Watching my young children race the waves and play in the water reminded me of my first experience with the ocean.

It felt like so long ago, but the fear that shot through my little body remained memorable to that day. I sat there watching my kids, thinking about that experience, thinking about how long it had been and how much life had changed. My thoughts eventually faded as I watched the waves crash and roll back out over and over. It seemed almost hypnotizing. Whenever I go to the beach, I am reminded of a saying that is written on several T-shirts, paintings, and signs around Newport: "Sometimes I sits and thinks, and sometimes I just sits."

The beach is such a relaxing place, full of sunshine, delicious food, and great company. Everyone seems to be happy and content. It is the pinnacle of carefree living. However, just beyond the sand castles, the boardwalk, and the good food is the ocean. The powerful and unpredictable ocean. So calm one day, but so destructive the next. Surfers often talk about developing a relationship with the ocean— knowing when to get in and when to get out. Yet even with a surfer's intuition, the ocean still feels so full of unknowns.

In many ways, the ocean is like life. Just as water may feel calm, controlled, and in balance, so too may our lives feel smooth and in control. But that same water that feels so calm and understood can quickly become a means of destruction. That same water can become a tsunami, hurricane, or riptide. Likewise, life can flip upside down pretty quickly. I guess it didn't take a tsunami to teach my seven-year-old self that water can be unpredictable and scary. However, I think it did take a tsunami to teach me those same lessons about life.

During the time of that vacation to the beach with my family, life was busy. I was almost ten years out of my endodontic residency training, and I was running a successful practice. My oldest son had just turned sixteen, and my youngest was only five. My kids were busy playing all kinds of sports, and I was coaching a couple of their teams. The rest of the time they were running off with their friends, so getting all of our family in the same place was becoming harder and harder. Luckily, as an endodontist, I had flexibility in my schedule, but life seemed to be moving faster every year. The beach was great because we all got to be together and take a week off from life. Unfortunately, the week flew by, but not before we filled it with delicious meals and fun days at the beach.

Our Family Vacation 2009
Left to right—John (16), Nate (10), Susan, Will (8), Charlie (5), Sarah (13)

On the second-to-last day of our vacation, we spent most of the day relaxing on the beach – racing waves, playing in the sand and tossing around any ball we could get our hands on. When the sun started to set, we called our kids back to us and told to them to gather their things. I stood up, turned and reached down to fold up my chair, but right as I grabbed hold of it, I felt a slight tingling feeling run through the left side of my body. I had felt it before, but it was stronger this time, and I was confused that it kept coming back.

I started the walk back to the beach house, opening and closing my left hand as I walked. My kids were off running around in the sand again, with smiles on their faces and no cares in the world. I anxiously waved to them to follow us. The tingling feeling had only stayed for a few seconds, but it left me feeling so uneasy that I couldn't think about anything else for the rest of the day. Later that night, I was lying in my bed with my mind racing while everyone had already fallen asleep. I had no idea what was causing this reoccurring sensation, but my curiosity and unrest got the best of me, so I decided to do some searching on the internet.

I pulled out my Blackberry and typed my symptoms into the search bar. After a few minutes of reading through potential causes of my symptoms, I threw my phone down, wanting to stay ignorant of any diagnosis. I tried to dismiss the possibility of this being serious and eased my conscience by blaming the symptoms on my young body getting older or being sore from working out. I knew the internet always makes things sound worse than they really are, but I still couldn't get the search results out of my mind. The results of any search I made describing my symptoms invariably came back suggesting that I see a doctor or a neurosurgeon. I told myself over and over that I was healthy and that this was just a minor symptom, but I knew I wouldn't be able to rest until I got myself looked at.

That night was spent tossing and turning until I finally decided to get up around five a.m. I drove to an empty parking lot a few miles from where we were staying. I was struggling to keep myself together, and those search results would not leave my mind. After sitting in the dark parking lot for several minutes, I decided to make a call. I called a close friend and neighbor, Chuck, who also happened to be a Harvard-trained neurosurgeon. I'm sure he was wondering what was going on when he saw that I was calling so early, but I couldn't wait any longer. He answered, "Hello, Dave?"

As soon as I heard his voice, I felt my throat tighten and the tears start coming. I could hardly get any words out. "Chuck. I think I might . . . I think I might have a brain tumor."

"What do you mean, Dave?"

I then described to him my symptoms, and he sighed. "Well, Dave, it's hard to make any concrete diagnosis without an MRI. It could be a lot of things. I wouldn't worry too much about it; it's probably nothing. Enjoy your vacation, and we'll take care of the MRI when you get back."

I hung up the phone, and the darkness surrounded me. What did this all mean? I was anxious and thought about trying to get an MRI in California, but decided to wait until we returned home. I knew that I shouldn't be upset without first getting an MRI, but deep down I felt like something was off. I reassured myself by ignoring what I had read and pretended like the tingling feelings were normal. I was a forty-year-old father of five. Life was good, everything was going smoothly, and I was not about to dismiss myself from life so soon. So I drove back to the beach house and tried my best to enjoy our final day in California.

DAVID KOELLIKER

Chapter 2

The MRI and Diagnosis

When we got back from vacation, I called in and made an appointment to get an MRI. Apparently, I wasn't the only person needing one, because it took about four weeks to get in. During those four weeks I tried not to think too much about everything, but that tingling feeling would come back every so often and remind me of its presence. I tried to stay busy but would frequently find myself preoccupied with thoughts about whatever was going on inside my body. It was like that feeling when you receive bad news, and no matter what you try to do to get your mind off everything, the gut-wrenching feeling keeps coming back.

Meanwhile, the rest of my life seemed to be going well. I had worked hard to build a strong endodontic practice in Salt Lake City, and I felt like I was at the peak of my career. I was precise and efficient in how I operated, and I had built relationships and friendships with many referring dentists in the area who would send me patients. My family had also just moved into a new house the year before and had built many friendships in our neighborhood.

When the time finally came to go in for the MRI, I remember feeling nervous as I laid down on what looked like a tanning bed. When you go in for a brain scan, you receive a dye through an IV that is designed to light up anything different in your brain. The tech started an IV, slid a hood over my face, put pillows on the side of my head and neck to keep me from moving, plugged my ears, and then started the machine.

It was my first MRI, so everything was a little foreign to me. They didn't really explain much about what was happening, but before I could ask any questions, the MRI was beginning. I couldn't help but feel badly for anyone with an ounce of claustrophobia. Not only was it a tight space, but it also made such a loud and bizarre pinging sound that made me feel like I was about to watch a rock and roll concert.

After about thirty minutes, the MRI came to an end, and the tech came in and pulled the hood and pillows off of my head and neck. She took out the IV but wasn't saying much. As I got up to leave, she politely said, "Well, I'm sorry; we will get the results to your doctor."

I said a quiet "thank you" as I walked out, but the only thing running through my head were her words: "I'm sorry." What was that supposed to mean? Were the results so clear they already knew what was wrong? Was the radiologist talking about the results out loud with my doctor on the phone? Did they think I already knew what was wrong with me? I was curious and sick to my stomach.

While I was driving home from the hospital, I got a call from my neurosurgeon. I answered quickly. "Chuck, do I have a brain tumor?"

He responded, "Well, Dave, we need to talk about it. Go to the baseball game, and then you and Susan come over to my house later tonight."

I knew something was wrong and wanted to ask him more, but decided to let it go and respect his wishes. Our sons played baseball on the same team, so he knew what our plans were for the evening. I hung up and started thinking about what this might mean, how bad it was, and what the next steps were. I wanted to call Chuck back and ask him a million questions, but again, I decided it would be best to wait. I called Susan and told her about the MRI and about my conversation with Chuck. She was obviously concerned but tried to stay positive and reassured me that everything would be okay.

After the baseball game ended, we went home, got the kids ready for bed, and slipped out of the house quietly. When we arrived at Chuck's home, just around the corner from ours, he greeted us politely and then took us to his small home office. I remember feeling so nervous I could hardly talk, but I waited patiently for Chuck to pull out his computer. We made small talk while he searched for the MRI scans, but the feeling in the room was disturbingly quiet. When he found the scan results, he turned his computer so that we could see and pointed towards a dark presence on the right side of my brain. "You see this? This dark mass right here? This . . . this is a brain tumor."

It was silent, and I went numb. Chuck outlined the tumor on the screen and continued, "Let's start with the good news." As if any good news could come immediately after hearing that you have a brain tumor.

"This tumor is in the safest part of your brain. The right temporal lobe is away from speech and personality centers and other parts that could significantly change who you are if they're damaged. It is also one of the more accessible parts of the brain during surgery. Unfortunately, the tumor is quite large, and we are going to have to operate." I felt emptiness and fear enter my body. I couldn't think or talk.

Chuck gave us a few seconds to process the news. I still couldn't believe what he had said. After a moment of silence, Susan asked, "How does this affect his life expectancy?"

Chuck responded, "It's hard to know exactly. More than likely this will shorten your life span. However, there are many people that live ten to twenty years with tumors like this. Don't get discouraged."

I was speechless. It was as if a lightning bolt had struck any words or feeling out of me. Don't get discouraged? With every word that was spoken, my life became more and more of a question. Nothing was certain. I didn't know how the tumor would affect my work, if I would die next month or in twenty years, or how this would affect the lives of my wife and five children. Just the way he had said "There are people who live ten to twenty years with tumors like this" made it seem like ten to twenty years was the best case scenario. Ten more years. That would be right after my youngest child turned fifteen years old. And that was the best case scenario? The only thing that was certain now was that my life was going to change.

Chuck talked to us more about the surgery that would take place, and we made plans to operate a few weeks from that night. He briefly explained the recovery process and the treatment schedule and told us that they would biopsy the tumor after the surgery so we could discover how aggressive it was. Depending on its severity, we would need to start chemotherapy and radiation shortly thereafter. He discussed various treatment options and potential complications associated with each treatment. Although surgery posed the highest threat of complication, it was clear that it was the best option. Much of what we talked about was a blur. I wanted to deny the seriousness of the situation because I had felt hardly any symptoms. I had biked fifteen miles that morning and worked a full day, my life was normal.

I was quiet for most of the conversation. I was fine letting Susan ask most of the questions and figure out the next steps. She was clicking into her action mode, something I always loved about her. She never backed down from a fight, and by the way she acted that night, I knew she most definitely wouldn't be backing down from this one.

After our conversation with Chuck, we thanked him and drove back home. Susan remained positive and kept reassuring me that everything would be okay. I didn't have much to say. I was still numb from the news, and my mind was refusing to process or accept what was happening. Neither of us shed a tear. We were past feeling. We had no idea what was to come, but we knew our lives would be changing significantly. Nothing was certain anymore.

Chapter 3

Mental Anguish

I woke up the next morning at 5:00 a.m., wondering if the previous day was just a bad dream or if it had really happened. The MRI and our conversation with Chuck had made this situation undeniably real, yet the absence of any significant symptoms made it hard to believe. Hearing Chuck talk about the seriousness of my tumor was so bizarre, because to me it seemed almost nonexistent. I was biking, lifting weights, running, and playing basketball several times a week, and I felt like my body was in good shape. My mind was sharp and everything seemed normal. But that's not what the MRI had said.

I knew that I needed to get out of bed so that I could clear my mind. I went downstairs and decided that I'd better call my parents, who were living in South Africa at the time. The phone rang a couple of times, and my mother answered. "David, you are calling so early. What's the matter?"

I guess mothers have a way of knowing exactly when something is wrong. As soon as I heard her voice, I felt the tears start coming, the same way a hurt child cries only once they can see their parents. "Mother . . . I have a brain tumor."

She responded, "Oh, David."

Just hearing her words made the tears flow harder and brought a gravity to the situation that hadn't been there previously. "They diagnosed it yesterday, and I'm going to need surgery."

No one likes making their mother upset. We continued talking about some of the things Chuck had told us—the location of the tumor, changes in life expectancy, next steps, etc. It was a difficult conversation. By that time, my father had started listening in. It felt like with every person I told, the more real my situation became.

When I went upstairs after the phone call, I was a wreck. It was still early, so none of the kids had woken up. Susan couldn't sleep either, and when I saw her, she had tears welling up in her eyes. The reality of the situation had set in. I told her that I was sorry and that I probably wouldn't be around to help her raise the kids for much longer. She told me that I didn't know that and that I shouldn't apologize. She told me to just stay positive. But it was hard. It's one thing to hear that you are going to die, but it's something entirely different to realize what that means for those you love—for those who depend on you.

My mind was spiraling downward. No longer would I get to watch my children grow up and get married. No longer would I get to meet and play with my grandchildren. No longer would I get to live a long life of retirement with my beautiful wife. Situations that I had never considered were thrust upon me as I thought about what this meant for my life and for the lives of those in my family. It was a never-ending pit of despair.

I needed to get out of the house, so I went over to my in-laws', who had asked us to take care of their house and yard while they were out of town. I began to water the plants, but the hopelessness of the news was almost too much to bear. I couldn't remember the last time I had cried before this whole thing started, yet now I couldn't stop the tears from coming. My mind was cycling through worries and fears without end. How do I tell my children? What does this mean for my career? How long do I have? And worst of all, if I die in the near future, who will take care of my children? I couldn't bear the idea of another man raising my children, my number-one responsibility and purpose in life. Although the answers were unknown, any scenario was significantly worse than before. These questions ate at me. With every new question, my despair amplified. I was in a dark place. Anguish and fear engulfed me.

As I stood in the backyard, watching the water flow out of the hose, I felt like there was no way out of this situation. I was distraught and spiraling down quickly. Just then, I heard a voice as clear and vibrant as someone standing right behind me.

"David. It's going to be okay."

I immediately recognized the voice as my sweet grandmother's. I turned around to face her, but no one was there. My grandmother had passed away only six months prior, so I don't know what I was expecting to see. Maybe it was instinct, or maybe I just wanted to see my Grandma Koelliker one more time. When I was growing up and went through what I thought were "tough times" in my adolescence, I would always go over to my grandmother's house and visit with her. She had such a peaceful and loving demeanor that could calm me down almost instantly. And there she came back to me at precisely the right moment. I needed her and she was there.

I had always been taught those we loved would look out for us on the other side, but in this moment those teachings became a reality. I know what some of you might be thinking. How could I possibly have heard her voice? It was probably just a figment of my imagination. Think what you must, but know this: this experience was more than just a fleeting thought. So clear was her voice that I turned around to see if she was there. There are plenty of things I don't know, but one thing I do know is that I heard my grandmother's voice that morning. It lifted me out of the hole my mind had been digging and sent a wave of peace and love through my body. That experience still reverberates with me as clearly as if it had happened yesterday.

Although the same difficult questions continued to cycle through my mind, I knew that the best thing to do would be to stay strong and fight this battle. I think many people misunderstand the phrase "fighting cancer." I know I probably did. But what I have learned is that the fight with cancer is not just a physical fight; the fight is in your mind. It is staying positive and determined, even when your physical body is taking a beating.

When someone dies from cancer, the fight isn't lost because their body was overtaken. The fight took place in their mind, heart, and soul. Victory is not determined by if or when they die, but how they lived while they were fighting. Cancer, like life, will do what it must, but we can control our attitude, how we treat others, how we live, and how we feel about ourselves and the world. Beating cancer shouldn't be about being cured from cancer; beating cancer should be about mentally and emotionally overcoming a difficult and sometimes terminal situation. It should be about living life to the fullest and being happy, even when everything seems to be pulling you the other way.

Hearing my grandmother's voice was the moment in time that I consider the beginning of my fight. It was when my grandma pulled me out of the miserable pit I was in, dusted me off, and told me that I'd be okay and

I'd better not quit. After that, I knew everything would be okay. Yes, it was tough to swallow a diagnosis that my life might end earlier than I had planned, especially with five kids, the oldest being sixteen and the youngest only being five. I had a family that needed me desperately. I was not going to give up physically, but I knew most definitely I could not give up mentally, spiritually, or emotionally. It would not make sense in my head, and it just didn't work for me. Regardless of whether I lived or died, I decided I was going to do my best to fight, serve, lift, help, and love those around me until the very end. I was going to focus less on how I was going to die and focus more on how I was going to live.

A few weeks later, I wrote the following in my journal:

> *I'm trying to understand why we and our loved ones have to suffer, and I found this thought:*
>
> *Elder Orson F. Whitney wrote: "No pain that we suffer, no trial that we experience is wasted. It ministers to our education, to the development of such qualities as patience, faith, fortitude and humility. All that we suffer and all that we endure, especially when we endure it patiently, builds up our characters, purifies our hearts, expands our souls, and makes us more tender and charitable, more worthy to be called the children of God . . . . and it is through sorrow and suffering, toil and tribulation, that we gain the education that we come here to acquire."*

I'm grateful that no one ever told me beforehand that in this fight I would lose most of my vision and my ability to drive, be forced to leave my job, endure chemotherapy and radiation, suffer a stroke and countless seizures, and undergo three brain surgeries. God probably knew the diagnosis was heavy enough for me at that time. The decision to take whatever life throws at you is much easier said than done. However, I decided even though my health was out of my control, there was still so much I could control. And I was going to do my best. My youngest child, Charlie, said it best: "Dad, you can either quit, or you can fight back." I knew it was time to fight.

Chapter 4

The Unknowns of a New Life

The surgery was scheduled for about three weeks after the MRI. I spent most of the time leading up to the surgery working at the office or on my knees in prayer. I spent a lot of time talking with God about how I should approach this, what I needed to learn, how I could find strength to make it through, how to tell my kids, etc. My kids were always on my mind. I didn't know how I should tell them what was happening, how much I should tell them, or how I should prepare them.

Every surgery has the potential for complications; however, brain surgery is interesting because complications could affect significant aspects of your life. Vision, speech, organization, moods, and even personality are all at risk. I didn't want to scare my children, but I also wanted them to know that I loved them in case something happened.

A few days before the surgery, I went to the Salt Lake City LDS temple, a peaceful place where I found an escape from life and a stronger connection with God. On this particular visit, I was looking for answers to my questions. I wanted to know what I was supposed to learn and how I could possibly make it through this experience. I prayed and prayed, but after two hours of praying and pondering, I was still without answers. I started thinking, "Susan is probably wondering where I am, and my car has probably been ticketed or towed."

Right as I was about to get up and leave, I received a strong impression. It came very clearly and very distinctly, like a flash of light or inspiration being sent from heaven. The impression was that I needed to submit my will to God's. Submit my will. What did that mean? I spent a lot of time thinking about that over the next week—and over the next several years. After a lot of thought, I think submitting my will simply means I needed to stop focusing on what I want.

Yeah, obviously I wanted to be healed. I wanted to be healed more than anything in the world. But I had this brain tumor for a reason, and complaining about it wasn't going to do anyone any good. I had always tried to be in control of my life, but there was no controlling a brain tumor. I was still going to fight. I was going to fight like crazy. But I also decided that no matter what happened, I was going to trust in God and forget about myself. The process of fully submitting is obviously difficult, but I've tried my best to do that ever since my experience in the temple. I've tried to stop being frustrated with my lack of control in this situation and work harder to use this experience to learn and help others.

I struggled with the idea that after this surgery, I might have significant side effects that would change my personality. In fact, the morning of the surgery I wrote a letter to my wife that said, "After this surgery you might have to fall back in love with the same guy you did in high school, before all of my schooling and training. I was just a brainless athlete who spent all of his time lifting weights."

Although I joked about it to make it seem less serious, I really hoped that wouldn't be the case. I also didn't want my kids to worry about me, and I definitely didn't want to scare them. With so many unknowns in the near future, I felt like talking about everything too much would just create more unknowns. Susan and I also decided to keep things only within our family. It was a burden that we preferred to keep private, and because so much was unknown, there really wasn't a lot to talk about. I visited or called all of my siblings and told them that I would be having a surgery to remove a tumor. They were all so loving and helpful and respected our wishes not to share the news. I told my kids that I just had a small "bump" inside my head and that our neighbor was going to do a "little" surgery to take it out. They didn't understand, and I preferred it that way.

As a deeply religious person, I also thought a lot about my preparation to meet my God. If this tumor was going to take me, I wanted to be mentally, emotionally, and spiritually prepared. I spent a lot of time thinking about my life and what I had learned. I prayed, fasted, and tried to understand why God wanted me to go through this experience. I tried to stay positive and strong, feeling confident that God would let me raise my children for a little while longer. I was not ready to leave them yet.

When I arrived to the hospital on the day of surgery, I was taken into the presurgical holding area. I was nervous but confident in the doctors. Chuck was the neurosurgeon performing the surgery, and the anesthesiologist was also a close friend of mine. These doctors were not only extremely well trained, but they were also some of my closest friends. I felt like a very blessed man to have so many good people operating on me. The nurses spent some time getting everything ready, and they got my IV all set up. After several minutes, they rolled my bed into another room. We made small talk along the way, and then everything went black as the anesthesia took its toll.

When I woke up from the surgery, I felt good. I was tired, but my mind seemed clear, and that was a relief. Susan and my dad were sitting on some chairs in my hospital room and were very happy that I was awake. A few moments later, Chuck came in to check on me. He asked me how I was feeling and was clearly pleased with my progress. I asked him how everything had gone, and my family listened as he told us about the surgery. Chuck said that the procedure had gone smoothly, but then he stopped and got very serious for a moment. He said something along the lines of this:

"Dave, the most interesting thing happened during your surgery. I felt like there was something directing me where to cut. It was as if the tumor was outlined for me and my scalpel knew exactly where to go. I don't know what it was, but I know I had unseen help during that surgery."

I was so grateful for Chuck that day, not only because he was an incredible surgeon, but because he lived his life in a way that merited whatever divine help he had received. It was one of the many not-so-small miracles I've witnessed along this journey.

I came home a few days after the surgery and spent the week resting and lying low. Rest is obviously important after a brain surgery, but I also knew that once I left the house, it would be difficult to hide my half-shaved and stapled head. I wore a baseball hat everywhere and tried to go unnoticed for a couple of weeks.

Undergoing this first major surgery had a profound impact on my life. It was the first significant event that I experienced as a result of the tumor, and it was a strong realization for me that this tumor was, in fact, real. It hit me hard. I always knew that life was precious, but now my own life was the one in question. This may sound drastic, but I really feel like my personality and the way I viewed the world changed. In many ways, I felt like I needed to be better. I needed to love people more.

Following the surgery, I instituted an unwritten rule with all of my friends and my children's friends that they would have to give me a hug whenever they came to visit. Every time they would walk through the door, I would say, "Only hugs in this house." I'm sure the neighborhood kids wondered why I started hugging them, but they caught on quick, and that motto has continued on even to this day. When friends or family come to visit, we give hugs. I knew that if I were going to die, the number-one thing I would want my friends, family, and neighbors to know was that I loved them.

Eventually, I started working again, and everything returned back to "normal." However, after a surgery like that, nothing ever fully returns to normal. I often wondered if mistakes I made were simply due to my own forgetful self or if they were a side effect of the tumor. My wife would send me to the store to buy turkey, and I would come home with ham. I would sit and wonder if I just had a bad memory, if that was the tumor, or if my mind was just preoccupied with other things. It was probably just a combination of everything. And honestly, I made mistakes like that all the time before my surgery, but I couldn't help but question if everything I did wrong had some tie to the tumor. My doctor told me not to worry and that everyone makes mistakes. He said it's common for patients to beat themselves up over things like that, but it probably had nothing to do with the tumor. It was frustrating though, and it made me nervous.

One of the more disappointing pieces of news we received in the weeks following the operation was that the tumor was positioned in a way that prevented it from being fully removed through surgery. This meant that the road to being tumor-free was far from being over. However, after running some tests, the doctors determined that the tumor was an astrocytoma with a mix of grade 2 and grade 3, meaning that it wasn't as aggressive as some tumors but still something to be careful about. I was happy that it wasn't grade 4 but knew the unfortunate reality that most grade 2 and 3 tumors eventually progress to something more serious.

The more I thought about everything going on, the more I realized how little control I had in all of this. I was trying my best to submit my will to God's, but it's so difficult to feel like your life is almost completely out of your control. Throughout my life, I had learned I could fix almost all of my problems through work, determination, money, forgiveness, love, or something else. But this tumor was different. Besides following doctors' counsel, taking my medication, and praying as often as possible, there weren't many other options, and that was a tough reality to face. However, even though I couldn't necessarily control the outcome of my health, there were many things I could control. My brain tumor brought so much fear and doubt into my life, but I've tried my best to eliminate those feelings and replace them with positivity and hope. I try to think about this as an opportunity.

My tumor $\neq$ fear and doubt   My tumor $=$ opportunity

My tumor is an opportunity to experience feelings, friendships, and love in a way that I have never experienced them. To enjoy every day. To break down the moments and take it all in. To appreciate the little things and be grateful for the people around me.

When you feel like your days are numbered, you start to consider big life questions. You start to wonder what really happens after this life. You think about your family and if you will be with them after you die. You wonder what your purpose on this earth really is. At church, I've learned about what will happen after this life, and I've learned I can be together with my family forever someday. I've also learned that my purpose in this life is to perfect myself. To learn how to be a better version of me—one day at a time.

I'm just like the next person—I need as much time as possible to learn how to be perfect, but the tumor is giving me less time. It has made me feel like I need to speed up the process. I'm almost certain that I won't get ninety years on this earth, and I might not even get fifty or sixty. This frightens me at times, but I also feel like it's an incredible opportunity. It pushes me to be better. I try to live every day like it's my last, because one of these days will most definitely be my last. And that day is coming soon.

This sense of urgency to be a better person, to be kinder to others, and to love more has changed my life. I obviously haven't been perfect. But I feel more sensitive to my mistakes. I feel like the innermost desires of my heart have changed.

This desire and will to be better has been a frequent topic on my mind since I was diagnosed. As a result, a thought that occurred to me early on in my fight with cancer was the relationship between the growth of my tumor and sin. I know it seems bizarre to think that my tumor was actually linked to being a good or bad person, but it has become very real to me the longer this fight goes on. Around that time, I wrote about this thought in my journal:

I have been wanting to write for some time now but haven't had the opportunity to organize my thoughts the way I have wanted. There have been many lessons learned over the past several years, and many continue to be learned, but one that has had particular poignancy is the relationship between my tumor and sin. I have felt that there is somehow a connection between the two, and the only one that understands it is me. Some may say, "No, you're being too hard on yourself" or "I don't understand what you mean." But every time I read accounts in the scriptures about sin and its effects on the soul, I realize that the interconnection is something no one else can understand but me.

Nephi said, "Why should I yield to sin, because of my flesh?" (2 Nephi 4:27). Every time I say an unkind word or react in anger, my thoughts turn to my tumor. It becomes larger figuratively. I lose hope and become frustrated with my condition. When it becomes larger figuratively, it grows physically. I know this is true because I don't sleep as well; I worry and let things of little consequence bother me. The relationship is startling. I could deny it and try to wish it away, but it won't do me any good. In a very literal sense, I die every time I sin. Later in verse 27, Nephi continues, "Yea, why should I give way to temptations, that the evil one have place in my heart to destroy my peace and afflict my soul?"

I can't express how difficult my life becomes when I do something that I know is wrong. My peace leaves. I think about it as I go to bed, when I wake up. My soul is literally afflicted. God cannot look upon sin with the least degree of allowance (D&C 1:31), and in a very real way I cannot either. I am not talking about grievous sins. If I were I would be dead. I am talking about the sins of pride and rudeness, speaking unkind words, or being easily offended. Those are the sins that so easily beset me and destroy my peace.

Nelsen Mandela had it right when he said, "Resentment is like drinking a poison and then hoping it will kill your enemies." Sin is poison to me. I drink poison. With that said, you can imagine how important the sacrament has become for me. "Oh God, the Eternal Father" is my cry every Sunday. It is my vaccine, my antidote. My soul is cleansed and purified once again. I can continue to live.

My hope is that "I shall be telling this with a sigh/ Somewhere ages and ages hence:/ two roads diverged in a yellow wood, and I—/ I took the one less traveled by,/ and that has made all the difference." I hope the Lord will grant me my desire to "shake at the appearance of sin" (2 Nephi 4:31) I will probably die from this tumor someday, but we all are terminally ill. My hope is that there will be no sting of regret associated with it. My faith is in the promise that

"Whatever principle of intelligence we attain unto in this life, it will rise with us in the resurrection" (D&C 130:18).

Therefore, I rejoice in the tribulation and the education. I have faith that the Lord would not place me in this circumstance and not give me the power to overcome it. I know it is true. I feel it every day, and when I am not feeling his power in my life I repent, because I know he is waiting to bless us. We are all beggars, and I am no exception.

I want to be clear that I am in no way suggesting that individuals with a tumor or disease were given those difficult conditions because they were bad people. Bad things happen to good people all the time, and that is unfortunately just the way it is. And I don't think that is why I got my tumor either. However, once I was diagnosed with the tumor, an almost incurable condition, I felt like my life was no longer in my hands. I needed God's help. I think many other cancer patients understand this feeling. When there isn't a known cure for your condition, your only hope is a miracle. And if you want a miracle, you want to feel confident about asking God for that miracle. And if you are constantly trying to be a better person, you develop more confidence in your relationship with God. You put your trust in a higher power, and that gives you hope. That's why I felt like my tumor was a tumor of sin. As I committed sin by being prideful or not treating others with kindness, my confidence that God would grant me a miracle decreased, and so did my hope of survival. As I strove to be a good person, my hope in a cure or extended life would increase. That feeling has encouraged me to be a better person and still gives me hope to this day.

Chapter 5

Good Doctors, Good Medicine

Life continued as usual after my surgery, and my symptoms were minimal. Without any pain or symptoms, it was easy to forget that I still had a brain tumor. It was like a reoccurring bad dream I tried to push out of my life by not thinking about it. This created a weird double-life feeling. In one of my lives, I was a father of five children, an endodontist, a little-league baseball coach, and someone who loved biking, hiking, and playing sports. The other person was the brain tumor patient. The discouraging reality of my second life would occasionally peek into my first life and make sure I remembered it. It was tough to accept, but probably healthy to remember. And, of course, MRIs were very good at reminding me that I didn't have two lives; I only had one.

After being diagnosed with this tumor, every time I would need to make an important life decision, I would first consult with an MRI. It never told me exactly what to do, but it helped me to know if I should continue down my chosen path or make an adjustment. In the fall of 2012, a few years after my first surgery, I was trying to decide if I should bring on an associate into my dental practice.

Typically, I would get an MRI two to three times a year, but I hadn't gone in for over five to six months, so I decided it might be a good idea to have another. So I called to schedule an appointment and went in for the MRI. Unfortunately, the results of the MRI showed that the tumor had grown, and it was time to consider another surgery. As I talked with my doctor about potential treatment options, I was so grateful that he listened to my concerns and genuinely wanted to help.

For many years, the standard treatment had been surgery, radiation, and chemotherapy. Although some tumors respond well to those treatments, many do not. Chuck wanted to give me the best opportunity to live, so he recommended that we look into a new clinical trial that was being done at UCLA. Although the words "clinical trial" brought a sense of risk with them, Susan and I were interested in any new technology or treatment available.

This MRI helped me make the decision to bring on an associate endodontist to my private practice. I knew that if the tumor was still growing, it would be good to have another endodontist in the practice who could take over if I needed to leave for a period of time. Plus, through a series of miraculous events, I met a wonderful, recently graduated endodontist wanting to practice in Utah. We went out for lunch, and it felt like we had been friends for years. He was the perfect fit for what I needed, and I like to think it was a good setup for him as well.

As Susan and I did more research on the clinical trial at UCLA, we discovered that my type of tumor was a great fit for the criteria they were looking for. We flew out to meet the doctor and were very impressed with her background and her plans for the trial. Her name is Dr. Liau. Dr. Liau lost her mother to a brain tumor when she was young and decided to dedicate her life to finding better ways to treat brain tumors. They say the decision to be a neurosurgeon is more of a calling than a career decision, and Dr. Liau clearly felt that call.

In one of our introductory meetings with Dr. Liau, she explained more clearly what would be done during the trial. My understanding of the hypothesis behind the trial was to use the body's natural immune system to identify and attack the tumor. Tumors are good at disguising themselves and can silently take over without resistance from the body. Patients in the clinical trial would undergo a surgery to remove as much of the tumor as possible. Following the surgery, the doctors would create a personalized vaccine made from the extracted tumor tissue. The patient would then receive the vaccine several times in the hopes that the body would learn to identify and fight off the tumor.

My wife and I decided to keep this surgery quiet as well. In fact, this time we only told my parents, my wife's parents, and my children (although we downplayed it again for my kids). My oldest child, John, was living in Brazil as a missionary at the time, and I struggled with knowing the best way of telling him the news. Missions were hard enough, and I didn't want to add any homesickness or stress to his life. So I decided to write him a letter about a month before the surgery, explaining the situation. I prayed that he would get the letter at a time that would be best for him. I later found out that he received it the day after my surgery. I'm sure that was a fun letter for him to receive.

It had been over three years since the first surgery, and Susan and I were hopeful that everything would go just as smoothly as the first time. I flew out to Los Angeles occasionally for pre-op appointments. Meeting with Dr. Liau and other staff helped to calm my nerves and prepare me for the upcoming surgery. After one of these appointments, I jotted this impression down:

> *As I sit in the UCLA waiting room and watch all of the people check-in for their appointments, I can't help but wonder if these people have all had the same experience I have had. This brain tumor ordeal, although there have been moments of extreme stress and anguish, has brought me closer to my Savior and my God. The thought occurred to me that the true blessing of my outcome has been exactly that.*

> *We can go through any experience in life—small or large, deeply*

*disappointing or wonderfully successful—and if it doesn't bring us
closer to our Savior, the experience isn't consecrated for our good.
Essentially, it's like depositing a large sum of money in a bank and
choosing the lowest interest rate possible. I want the highest interest
rate possible in the Lord's bank. I want all of my experiences to be
consecrated for as much good as the Lord sees fit.*

I still feel that way. I'm sure my "interest rate" has fluctuated at times
throughout this ordeal, but I've tried to keep a positive attitude and learn
as much as I can from this experience.

When the time finally came to fly out to Los Angeles for the surgery, we
decided to not book any patients in my office for three weeks after my
surgery. Dr. Sadler, my associate, would take any emergencies and could
cover a reduced flow of patients during that time. My kids would
continue to go to school, and my sister came over to watch them at
night. Susan and I left quietly and told them we were heading out on a
little trip to Los Angeles. My dad also came out with us and stayed in
UCLA student housing.

When we arrived at the hospital, we checked-in and were taken to their
surgical holding area. They wrote a big "Yes" on the right side of my
head to indicate which side of my head they would be opening up. I
guess if that was what it took to open up the right side, then it works for
me. I'd prefer a big "NO!" by the tumor, but I guess we'll take a "Yes"
for "Yes, please get this out of my head."

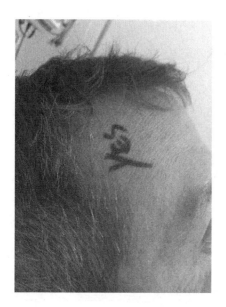
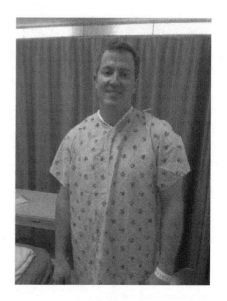

The nurses started the IVs, and everything went black again. After about five hours in surgery, I was wheeled into my hospital recovery room, and Susan was ushered in too. The surgery went well, and it was so great to wake up to my sweet wife by my side. She told me that for the past couple of hours I'd been very groggy and had been touching her hand saying, "I love the touch, I love the touch." I guess I'm glad I didn't say anything more embarrassing. I do love her touch

Dr. Liau came into the room after a few hours and told us that the surgery had gone very smoothly. In fact, she said that as they opened up my skull, it felt like the tumor was wanting to come out on its own. After a week in the hospital and a week resting at the hotel, I came home with another giant twenty-two-staple horseshoe scar on the right side of my head.

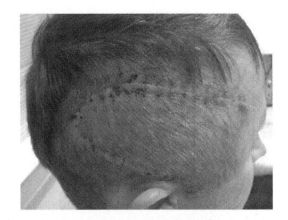

I did have a few new symptoms after this surgery, the most significant involving my vision. For the next three weeks, I think my glasses prescription changed every day, and it was always accompanied by double vision. I broke the bank by buying three pairs of glasses in the first three weeks but finally just decided to wait until my vision stopped changing.

This brought headaches and dizziness, but my vision eventually went almost back to normal. The one aspect of my vision that never returned to normal was the left-side field cut that I began to develop after the second surgery. My eyes could still see everything on the left side, but my brain didn't always process it. It wasn't a huge issue at the time; my kids would just call it the "dark zone." The dark zone was very small, and I could still play catch, work, and do everything normally. It did make it more difficult to see the golf ball off my club, but that's probably because I hit the golf ball all over the place.

About two weeks after the surgery, my family and I flew to Florida for a week. We wanted to allow my scar time to heal and let my hair grow back a little bit before we went back to Utah and continued on with our lives. I had recovered so quickly from the first surgery, and I made the mistake of thinking that I could treat the recovery of my second surgery the same. Each surgery has its own outcome and complications. Dr. Liau had recommended that I abstain from any exercise or intense physical activity for at least a month.

On one of the days that we were in Florida, Susan decided to take the kids to Disney World so that I could stay at the hotel and rest. At this point in time, my vision was still changing drastically every day, and it was driving me crazy. I was seeing double and everything was blurry. I decided to leave the condo to find an optometrist. I put on a hat and went down to ask the concierge where the nearest optometrist was. I was informed it was down the road and was asked if I wanted a taxi. I decided to walk because I wanted a little exercise.

What I didn't understand was that the optometrist was almost five miles away. I was seeing double, my family was all at Disney World, it was over ninety-five degrees, and I had a giant scar on the side of my head. I started the walk with plenty of energy but quickly began to realize that I was much farther away than I had anticipated. I finally made it to the office completely exhausted, dehydrated, and overheated.

One thing I have discovered throughout this entire experience with a brain tumor is that there are unexpected angels, both seen and unseen, who have protected and helped me. The optometrist was one of those.

When I finally arrived and sat down in his office, he began to ask about my situation. He was so kind and understanding and wanted to do anything he could to help.

Eventually, after a lot of trial and error, he got me a new prescription for my glasses. After seeing his face when I told him how far I had come, I knew Susan's reaction would be even worse. He offered to drive me back to the hotel in his car, and I gladly took him up on that. I passed out asleep for the rest of the day and night. I was right about my Susan's face when I eventually told her where I had been. She was definitely upset with me, but I guess we were both just grateful that I didn't get hit by a car, faint, get heat stroke, or have something else happen. Probably not smart to walk in the blazing Florida heat only two weeks after a massive brain surgery. I don't think Susan has ever forgiven me for that afternoon.

Reflecting on my experience with Dr. Liau at UCLA, I am so grateful for the opportunity to participate in the development of cutting-edge technology for brain tumor treatment. The clinical trial never fully removed my tumor, but I met incredible people along the way and hope that this trial contributes to saving lives in the future.

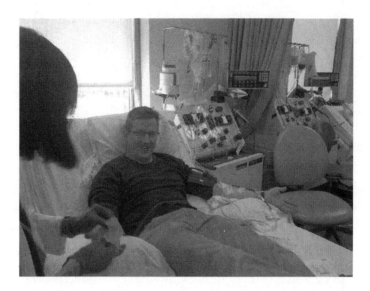

Returning to UCLA to receive treatments post-surgery

Chapter 6

New Symptoms, New Growth

After recovering for a few weeks, I went back to work again, and life went back to normal (besides the fact that I had a partially shaved head and a massive scar). Covering my healing scar was always exciting. Susan would sprinkle artificial hair on the right side of my head, and I would wear hats wherever I possibly could. I even went to watch my future daughter-in-law, Karli, dance at Cougarettes in Concert while I was wearing a baseball hat. I'm sure everyone thought I was disrespectful, but that was better than the looks I would get if they saw my scar.

I flew back to Los Angeles every three weeks for the vaccine (or a sugar pill placebo) and continued that over the following three months. My vision also stabilized, and I was cleared to exercise regularly. I had high hopes the tumor would respond positively to the vaccine, but I realized there was no way of knowing what was on the tumor's agenda. We eventually got the results back from the biopsy of the tumor and discovered that it was still a mix of grade 2 and grade 3. It had grown significantly since the first surgery, but luckily it hadn't progressed to a grade 4 tumor yet. However, my doctor warned me that, due to the location of the tumor in my right temporal lobe, I was at risk for seizures.

That risk became a reality when I was at my son's baseball game in April of 2014. It had been over a year since the surgery at UCLA, and I hadn't noticed any major symptoms. So I kept pushing myself like I always had. As a father of five, I was accustomed to functioning on little sleep, but I should have known that the tumor wouldn't allow me to go at the same pace I was used to.

My son's game was on a Friday morning in St. George, Utah, about five hours south of our home in Salt Lake City. I had been working hard all week but wanted to be there for his first game in the morning. To get there on time, I woke up around 2:00am to start the trek. After four and half hours of driving, I pulled up to the field, and walked over to the grandstands where the other players' parents were sitting. I said hello to everyone and sat down next to a friend, who offered me some sunflower seeds. I took the bag of seeds, grabbed a handful, threw them in my mouth, and then everything went black.

I woke up in the ambulance with my son, Nate, looking at me. He was still in his baseball uniform, and we were on our way to the hospital.

Without really knowing what was going on, I told him that I was sorry and that I was going to be okay. From his facial expression, I could tell he didn't really believe me.

When we got to the hospital, they ran some tests to make sure that I was stable and then took an MRI. The friend I had sat next to at the baseball game had come to the hospital and called my wife to tell her what happened. Apparently, I had blacked out and had a seizure. Another fan at the baseball game, who was a doctor, ran over to me and made sure I was okay.

Considering that at this point in time, no one outside of my family knew about the brain tumor, I think all of our friends at the game were surprised and confused. My wife flew down to St. George, and we eventually left the hospital. The next day, my wife drove us back to Salt Lake City. Driving after a seizure is very dangerous, so I was glad to have her with me. The likelihood of having a second seizure is very high within one to two months after the first seizure, and the last place you want that happening is behind the wheel.

After that experience, I tried to get more rest and be careful to not overwork myself. I also went in for a checkup with my doctor, and was told I shouldn't drive for three months. Members of my family took turns driving me to work in the morning. It was frustrating to depend on others for transportation, but I enjoyed being able to spend some extra time with my kids, wife, siblings, and parents. It was a rare opportunity to talk with my children without them being able to escape, so I tried to embrace it. This was the first taste of the dependence on others that would one day become a significant part of my life.

Another bizarre side effect of the tumor was that I would frequently experience *déjà vu*. I would be driving down the street, talking with a friend, or walking our dog, and would feel like I had been there or done that before. *Déjà vu* is always a strange feeling, but it was happening frequently enough to notice a difference. Every week I would have several feelings and experiences with *déjà vu*. I wish I knew what caused it, but the only response I got from doctors and the internet was that it was a common side effect in many brain tumor patients. I've also read that *déjà vu* is frequently associated with seizures, so every time it happened, I would get worried that it meant a seizure was in my near future.

I later learned more about seizures and the various forms they can come in. The seizure at the baseball game was called a grand mal seizure. I lost consciousness and started shaking, and it was obviously a more serious form of seizure. However, I also learned the tingling feelings that had occurred several times were called petit mal seizures. Much less disruptive, but still alarming.

I experienced several petit mal seizures but always tried to get some rest as soon as I could in order to prevent something worse from happening. I had a second grand mal seizure about a year after the one at the baseball game. Luckily I was at home, but my son Will happened to be there, and I think I scared him half to death. I hated that the tumor caused so much stress and fear for my children and my wife. I tried to protect them from it, but when I had seizures, there wasn't really anything I could do. I had always tried to be a foundation of strength for my family, but moments of physical weakness were becoming more and more frequent.

Every time something like this would happen, I would feel despair and fear creep into my thoughts. I'd get a feeling of helplessness, a feeling that my life was coming to an end, and I wasn't ready. I hadn't done what I wanted to do, and I hadn't become the man that I wanted and needed to be. Seizures weren't the only things that triggered those dark thoughts. Sometimes they would come when I was tired, after I had been rude to someone, or after an MRI.

Usually, whatever triggered those thoughts was insignificant, but once I started dwelling on my fear, doubt, and despair, it was hard to shake. Sometimes these feelings would stay for just a night and sometimes for several weeks, but regardless of how long they stayed, the feelings would consume my every thought and discourage me. I'd do everything I could to push them out, because I knew these thoughts wouldn't do any good, but it was tough. I wrote about it one time in my journal:

My fears and doubts are always greater at night. They are like dark shadows that lurk in the empty spaces of my head, ready to thwart my faith at any chance I give them. I give them a chance when I commit sin. When I'm sharp with one of my children or inconsiderate of my sweetheart. Those fears and doubts wake me up and unsettle me. Why can't I be more like Nephi and "shake at the appearance of sin"? Why am I so easily tripped up and thrown off course? Why do I give place for the enemy of my soul? Perfection seems to be this illusion. It's like a pool of cold, refreshing water way off in the distance when I'm traveling through the desert. It seems to move the same distance away from me as I strive to get closer. Will I ever arrive?

What is perfection in this life? Is it continuing faithful throughout the journey? Never giving up? Rising each time I fall? Will I ever have any of my faults buried, never to return? I have been told that I have the power to overcome sin, transgression, and temptation. Does that mean that I have the power to be perfect? I know that with the Savior all things are possible. Does everyone have that power, a gift to all mankind?

Chapter 7

Being Stripped of Everything

As time went on, my health remained fairly steady, with only the occasional hiccup. Work was going well, and Dr. Sadler, the associate I had brought on, had become a really good friend. In February of 2016, I was trying to make the decision of whether I should form a partnership with him or if we should just continue on the same path we were going. I really liked Dr. Sadler, and although I had initially been opposed to forming a partnership, he was the kind of person—both in character and talent—that I would consider partnering with. So as I did with all big decisions, I decided to get an MRI to help me come to a conclusion.

When I went in for the MRI, I didn't get the news I wanted. The tumor had grown significantly again, and the doctors thought that some parts of the tumor were looking more aggressive, possibly grade 4. Grade 4 meant that my astrocytoma brain tumor was becoming a glioblastoma, or what some doctors call a "GBM." GBMs are known as the most aggressive and deadly forms of brain tumors. They are highly malignant because the cells reproduce quickly and are supported by a large network of blood vessels. Your body essentially fuels the tumor's growth, and then the tumor takes your body down.

The doctor recommended that we try chemotherapy and radiation, as we had only tried surgery up to that point. I had always been hesitant to jump into chemo and radiation because it meant more significant changes to our lives. Besides the nasty side effects, including nausea, hair loss, constipation, and weight loss, it could also slow cognitive ability, memory, and speech. It also meant that everyone would know about my situation, creating problems for work. Who wants to undergo a root canal surgery by a dentist who has a brain tumor? Even if I maintained the same coordination and skill as before, any little mistake might be attributed to the tumor, and I would be blamed.

For all of these reasons, and others, I knew that chemotherapy and radiation might force me to sell my practice. So the decision to proceed was a difficult one. But because chemotherapy and radiation are considered the "standard of care," I needed to try them before I would be permitted to join any other studies or trials. Considering that we had exhausted our other treatment options, it was the only clear path.

The next few months were spent in preparation for the changes that would come with chemotherapy and radiation. The decision whether or not to form a partnership with Dr. Sadler became a decision of whether to form a partnership or just sell my practice to him outright, and retire as a practicing endodontist. This decision was one of the most difficult I ever faced. I had trained and worked my entire life to be an endodontist, and I was at the prime of my career. I would work four busy days during the week, be home by 5:00 p.m., and take Fridays off. I had built strong relationships with referring dentists, and I was one of only a handful of board-certified endodontists in the area. Everything seemed to be going great, but once again, the tumor had other plans—always helping me learn to submit my will.

After talking with my wife and considering how this might impact our lives, we made the decision to sell my practice. I vividly remember the week I made that decision. I couldn't sleep. Five nights in a row, I woke up in the middle of the night and went downstairs to my little office in our storage room. It wasn't just that I had to quit work; it was that I felt like this tumor was slowly stripping me of everything I loved. One thing at a time.

On the last of those five nights, as I was crying and feeling overwhelmed with everything going on, I remember a thought that came clearly to my mind: "Dave, what is your problem? Other people can fix teeth. What you need to be is a dad."

It hit me hard. And I couldn't stop thinking about it for a long while. But it helped me to reevaluate what my purpose on this earth really was. It wasn't to be an endodontist. It was to be a husband and a dad.

Once the decision had been made, I never looked back. I knew second-guessing my decision would only make things harder. I talked to Dr. Sadler, and everything fell into place for him to purchase and take over the practice. The smoothness of the transition confirmed our decision. I've learned when something falls into place in your life, it's best to just go with it. However, there was one last thing I wanted to do before giving up my life as an endodontist. I'd been invited to speak at the National Endodontic Conference in San Francisco in early April. Susan and I booked our flights and scheduled my first dose of chemotherapy and appointment for radiation for the Monday following the conference.

The conference eventually came, I flew out to San Francisco, and the presentation went well. My brothers and parents flew out to watch, which really meant a lot to me. It was a great way to finish my career as a practicing endodontist. Luckily, I had received an offer to work at the dental school at the University of Utah, so I was looking forward to remaining in my chosen field, even though I wouldn't be running my own practice.

When we returned home from the conference on a Sunday evening, I got ready to start my cancer treatment. The plan was to undergo six weeks of intense chemotherapy and radiation, followed by four months of more sporadic doses of chemo and less frequent visits for radiation. During the first six weeks I would take a chemo pill every single night and would go in for radiation appointments every weekday.

For my situation, the doctors decided that it was best for me to take chemotherapy orally through a pill. They told me that taking these pills would help the treatment to cross the blood-brain barrier. I was shocked to learn that I wasn't allowed to touch the pills with my bare hands. The medicine bottle had instructions to use a glove when holding the pills. I thought it was interesting—I couldn't touch the pill, but I was supposed to swallow it? Oh well. I used gloves for the first week, but after that I figured if it was going into my stomach, I could touch it with my hands.

The first night of chemotherapy, I decided to take the pill without any anti-nausea medication. I didn't want to take it unless I knew that I needed it. My doctor had recommended that I take it, but I decided to hold off to see how I felt. Ten minutes after taking my first chemo pill, I began throwing up. The entire night was spent looking into a toilet bowl, throwing up whatever I had left in my body. That was my first experience with chemotherapy.

The first time I went in for my radiation appointment, they made a plastic mask that was used to keep my head in the exact same position for every appointment. They then strapped me down on a big machine and used laser technology to identify where they should direct the radiation.

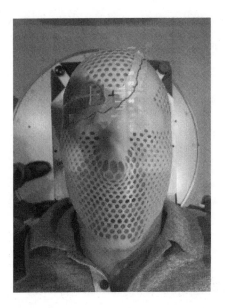 

Every time I went in for a radiation appointment, I would feel tired and sick for the rest of the day. Combine that with chemotherapy, and I had hair loss, constipation, a dry mouth, loss of taste sensors, dulled thinking, and constant exhaustion. After the first three weeks of this treatment, I was able to pull out clumps of hair. I would wake up in the morning with heaps of hair on my pillow. After these disgusting experiences, I decided to shave my head.

I also began taking the anti-nausea medication the doctor had recommended with my chemo pills. This eased the sick feeling a little bit, but I still managed to lose thirty-five to forty pounds in about three months of treatment. I'm sure the first fifteen pounds were good to lose, but then I started looking sickly skinny and losing a lot of my muscle.

My favorite part of going through this treatment process was working with all of the amazing doctors, nurses, and hospital administrators along the way. There were so many intelligent people who worked so hard to help me and make sure I was getting the best treatment possible. However, beyond just being intelligent, these individuals were good people. They had seen how cancer affected patient after patient, and I think that gave them an added level of empathy and compassion.

I would ring the "celebrate" bell every day after finishing radiation

As I continued on with my treatment, there were a few symptoms that began to get worse. The most significant of those symptoms was the left-side vision field cut. While this wasn't too big of a deal for most everyday tasks, it did cause some problems behind the wheel. In a matter of two weeks, I rear-ended someone as I changed lanes, ran into a pillar in an underground parking garage, and heard countless variations of the F-word, accompanied by several "friendly" hand gestures.

In fact, one of those instances was recorded on a voicemail I left for my oldest son, John. I was calling to see how his day went while I was in the car and must have almost hit a woman walking across the street at night. Right as I was about to leave a voicemail, the woman started yelling at me, and we caught her obscenities and my apologies all on voicemail.

Another bad driving experience happened when I pulled up to a stoplight and a woman pulled up next to me on my right side. She rolled down her window and with both middle fingers in the air yelled, "GET THE F&%$ OFF THE ROAD!" It was surprising, as I had literally no idea what had happened, but her anger was so intense that it startled me. I knew it was probably time for me to take that woman's advice.

My wife had been encouraging me to stop driving, and these events made me realize that it was probably best. The last thing I wanted was to hurt or kill someone else before this tumor killed me. So I decided to stop driving. Not being able to get around, especially in a highly residential area where we live, was such a debilitating feeling. It was another significant blow to my independence. I never realized how nice it was to be able to listen to music or audiobooks by myself as I drove around. More than anything, I hated feeling like a burden to those around me. Any time I wanted to get something for our house, to buy my wife flowers, or to go to lunch with a friend, I had to ask for a ride.

As the word got out that I had stopped working and was going through chemotherapy and radiation, we started seeing an influx of neighbors and friends come by our house to see how they could help. My kids couldn't walk down the street without being stopped by four or five people wanting to know about everything going on. It wasn't nosy or malicious; it was out of genuine concern for our well-being, but I know it was exhausting for them.

We quickly realized that one of the hardest parts of being diagnosed with something so serious is you constantly feel like you are bringing others bad news. Over time, it almost becomes difficult to have a conversation that doesn't involve talking about your well-being and health challenges. And with the seriousness of a brain tumor, you rarely ever get to tell people you are cured. The conversation would almost always result in this backwards situation with us having to comfort everyone we talked to, telling them that we would be okay and that we would keep chugging along one day at a time. It's not their fault, everyone wants to hear a comeback story. It's just hard that my story slowly gets worse and worse.

After starting chemotherapy and radiation, my hair was gone, I was losing weight like crazy, and everybody knew about our situation. However, even though it was sometimes overwhelming to have to talk about my tumor every time we saw someone, we were also overwhelmed with love and kindness shown by our friends and family. It has been amazing to see the neighborhood rally around our family. Words cannot express how grateful we are for the love we've been shown and for the many quiet acts of kindness that people have done for us.

So many days we come home to a porch full of flowers and food. There have been so many kind texts. So many handwritten letters. Sometimes the letters feel like people are saying goodbye to me. They thank me for changing their lives or for helping them one time. I think people want to get everything out in case they don't ever get the chance to express their gratitude. I try not to let those types of letters bother me. I understand that it's hard to know what to do or say. I've never been very good at it either. It has interesting to be on the other side, though. Honestly, I'm just so grateful to be the recipient of so much kindness.

With such amazing technology and access to the resources we have, it is pretty amazing that we haven't found a cure for so many types of cancers. But there are so many lessons learned through cancer that I think we might miss if it were gone. My relationships with family and friends have been so much stronger and better since this brain tumor. Can you imagine if on the day of my diagnosis, I could have just taken a quick pill that healed me? Yeah, I would love to be with my family without wondering how much more time I have. But I feel like I would have missed out on so much. I wouldn't have needed as much faith, I wouldn't have seen so much kindness, I wouldn't have seen so much love. I know it sounds weird, but cancer can bring out the best in people. It breaks down the competition we feel in life and helps us realize how much we depend on each other. Something about interacting with people who are suffering or going through tough times helps us to forget about trivial things. It's a good feeling to depend on each other. It makes our lives more meaningful. I'm a blessed man to have so many good people in my life.

Left to right—Charlie (12), Nate (17), Sarah (20), Susan, Me, my daughter-in-law
Karli, John (23), Will (15)

Chapter 8

Knocking on Death's Door

Every time I went in for an MRI, I felt like I was going in for judgment day. I never wanted to show up at an MRI without feeling emotionally, spiritually, or mentally prepared, because I never knew what news I might hear on that day. Regardless of the news I heard, it always reminded me that my life was precious and that I needed to be ready to meet my maker. So I always tried to be ready and brace myself whenever it came time for an MRI.

In September of 2016, I went in for another MRI to see what progress had been made throughout chemotherapy and radiation. This was an MRI that I will never forget, because it was probably one of the worst I had ever had. The tumor had grown quite significantly and did not seem to be slowing down. It was hard to tell if the mass was made up of necrotic tissue that had died during radiation, if it was swollen, or if it was growing rapidly. The doctors thought it was probably a combination of all three, but the only way to find out was through surgery. They recommended that we go in for a third operation, because they felt like it would give me the most time. So we agreed and planned the surgery for the following week. They said we shouldn't wait any longer than that.

One of the most interesting aspects of modern medicine and standard of treatments is how they measure success based on time. The goal is always to extend your time. Outside of the medical world, we think of problems as being fixed or broken, unsolved or solved, cured or uncured. But that isn't how doctors think about it. In their eyes, we are all just living with a finite number of days left. The amount of days remaining is determined by God, our decisions, prior health, and medical treatment, so a doctor's goal is to influence those days for the better. In other words, we are all terminally ill, and the purpose of a doctor is to improve both the quality and quantity of days we have left. Maybe that's why I remember walking out of that meeting with such a terrible feeling. We always tried to stay so positive and hopeful, but it is hard when you hear they are running out of things to do to "extend your time."

My children and parents knew that I was going in for an MRI, so I called them to tell them what we had heard from the doctors. Those were tough calls to make. No one wanted to hear that the tumor had grown back, but again, I got to be the guy who always had bad news. I especially didn't like telling my children. My older children knew most of what was going on, so it was difficult to dull it down for them, but I always tried to sugarcoat the news for my younger children. However, at this point, even they were tough to fool.

I knew that the tumor was growing, because for the first time, my left side started feeling significantly weaker. I would grab my phone with my left hand and it would fall to the ground. I also kept hitting my head on the left side because I wouldn't see a wall, a door, or a hanging tree branch. It was so frustrating, and I know it made my family nervous. It got especially bad the Friday before the surgery was scheduled. I hit my head on the trunk door of our car and on our kitchen cabinets. My wife kept telling my son and daughter that I seemed "off" or "different" that day. But the deterioration was gradual enough that they didn't think to call my neurosurgeon.

The next day, Saturday, two days before the scheduled surgery, I went on a hike with my wife; my son John; and my daughter, Sarah. It was the Living Room hike in the mountains near Salt Lake City, and one that our family had done many times. But this time it was different. I was having a hard time walking along the path. I would slip often or walk into the bushes on the left side. Finally, I just grabbed onto my son's shoulders and used him to help me get up and down. I used to do this hike so easily, but it was uncomfortably difficult that day, and when we finally made it down the hill and drove home, it felt like the car was filled with silent worry for my well-being.

After lunch, I decided to go downtown to the Salt Lake City LDS temple with Sarah and John. We parked and started walking over to the entrance. We stopped to say hello to my homeless friend Evelin, who was always in the same place on the street asking for money. I volunteered in the temple every Thursday, and Evelin was always there after my shift. I had never given her any money, but I had done some dental work on her and often made her a lunch or brought her school clothes for her kids. She had suffered through a difficult family and financial situation, and she lived at the homeless shelter with her two children. On this particular day, we asked if she was hungry and she said yes. We told her we were going to the temple, but that we would pick her up some food right after we got out.

As we walked into the front entrance area of the temple, my body went numb, and I stumbled backwards and fell to the ground. The entrance of the temple had only a thin layer of carpet, and I hit my head really hard. My daughter screamed as I fell, and my son rushed over right as I began having a seizure. He loosened up my tie and my belt, just as a crowd began to form around us. I had given my family strict instructions not to call the ambulance after seizures, because most of the time I just needed to go home and rest. They always countered by saying that if I wasn't awake to tell them what to do in the moment, then they got to decide. Due to my surgery being scheduled for only a few days later, my kids immediately called an ambulance. And luckily, a couple was visiting the temple who happened to be a doctor and a nurse. They rushed over almost immediately after I fell.

After about twenty seconds, I came to, but didn't feel normal. I told my son that I felt off and that he needed to call Chuck. Every few seconds I would have another mini seizure, and the doctor who had come to assist my children said this was very unusual. I kept wanting to sit up and then lie back down, and everything just felt weird. Eventually, the ambulance arrived, and the paramedics came into the temple with a stretcher. I was stable at this point, but still not feeling very normal. They loaded me into the ambulance and headed out to Intermountain Medical Center, about twenty minutes away. The ambulance did not turn on the lights and sirens, which we learned was only for serious life-and-death situations. It's safer for ambulances and for other cars if ambulances drive at a normal pace, unless the individual needs those extra few minutes at the hospital in order to survive. Sarah followed behind us in our car and John rode with the paramedics in the ambulance.

About five miles before we arrived at the hospital, I began vomiting uncontrollably. My body had been able to handle a seizure and hitting my head on the ground, but the additional pressure in my head from vomiting was too much, so my body went unresponsive. I'm sure it really scared my son when the paramedics yelled to the ambulance driver, "Light 'em up!" and he turned on the lights and sirens for the final stretch before arriving at the hospital.

Susan and my son William were already at the hospital when we arrived. I had vomit all over my face and shirt and was partially falling off the stretcher as they rushed me in. I did not look good. The paramedics rushed me into the hospital and brought me into a room full of doctors and nurses. At one point there were probably eight to ten people running in and out of the room. They cut off all of my clothing, and because I had aspirated my vomit, they put in a breathing tube.

From what I heard, this hour was probably the worst of my family's lives. I was still unresponsive, and once the neurosurgeon arrived at the hospital, he decided I should be taken back for a CAT scan. By that time, all of my children, my parents, and some of my siblings had arrived at the hospital. There were lots of tears, and no one wanted to say much. The seriousness with which the doctors and nurses were doing everything communicated the gravity of the situation.

Right before they took me back for the CAT scan, the medical personnel allowed my kids and wife into the room for a quick blessing. I obviously wasn't awake for the blessing, but later heard that my son blessed me to fight through what was happening and regain consciousness. It was a very short blessing, but it came from the heart, and it was a desperate cry to the heavens for help. I was rushed back to the CAT scan room, and my entire family waited in the hall for whatever news was coming.

The results of the CAT scan came back a few minutes later, and luckily there was only minor brain bleeding. It seemed like the tumor was at least somewhat stable, so the doctors decided not to operate immediately. It's always better to wait for an MRI before operating, because the doctors would be able to sync my head with the computer and provide assistance to the surgeons. They decided it would be best to operate the next morning.

I was wheeled up to a room in the ICU and had all sorts of wires, IVs, and monitors hooked up to me. Nurses were constantly in and out of the room, checking on me and making sure I remained stable. I was taken back for the MRI and had every other test done that was needed for the surgery. Before everyone left for the night, my family had a group prayer. I wasn't conscious, but I know those prayers made a difference. Afterwards, my sweet wife decided to stay the night, and my son took everyone home. From what I heard later, it was a somber evening at home.

The operation took place the following morning, and my family received word that everything had gone as planned. There was a lot of tumor tissue and necrosis to cut out of my head, and the doctors hoped that it would relieve some of the pressure in my skull. However, the surgeons explained to my family that the state in which patients enter surgery is the

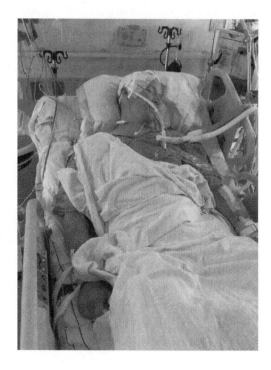

state that they come out. I continued to be hooked up to dozens of monitors, cords, IVs, and machines. My family thought the worst of all of them was the breathing tube, but luckily I don't remember much of that. I had the breathing tube in for about two or three days before they declared me free to breath on my own. Personally, I felt like the feeding tube was the worst of all of them. They stuck it through my nose and pumped my stomach full of gooey brown mush throughout the day.

The day after the surgery, my family and doctors were nervous that I didn't seem to be coming back to normal very quickly. I had basically slept for three days, and whenever I was awake, I wasn't alert at all. They had me hooked up to so many wires, tubes, and machines, and I kept wanting to pull them off of me. In fact, they had to strap my right hand and my chest down so that I wouldn't reach up to pull anything off. I think that was tough for my family to watch. I would fight with the straps, tug on them, pull on them, and do anything to get untied. It was like watching someone in a straitjacket struggle.

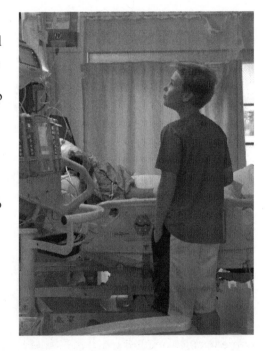

The nurses agreed to let my family untie me, so long as there was someone there to hold my hand so I didn't try to pull out my catheter, breathing tube, or feeding tube. There was one night that I was struggling to get my hand untied, and my son came over to untie me and hold my hand. Apparently, as soon as he untied me, I started reaching my arm up toward my face. Just when they thought I was going to grab hold of the tubes and pull them out, I put one finger on my forehead and scratched my face. My family laughed and wondered how long I had been wanting to itch my face but couldn't get my hand free to do it.

The PA and nurses would run tests every few hours to check my cognitive state, and in those first few days after the surgery, I didn't do too well on those tests. The most alarming part of the tests was that I wasn't able to feel or move anything on my left side. They would grab my right hand and say, "David, please squeeze my hand." And I would squeeze their hand. Then they would grab my left hand and say again, "David, please squeeze my hand." And my left hand would remain limp. Then they would say, "David, please wiggle your toes on your right foot." And I would wiggle the toes on my right foot. And then they would say, "Now David, wiggle the toes on your left foot." And I would wiggle my toes on my right foot, but the left remained still.

The part of the test that gave my family the most hope that I would come back to being the dad they knew was the smile test. After asking me to squeeze their hands, wiggle my toes, or match the number of fingers they were holding up, they were always disappointed that I didn't seem to be doing very well. But when they said, "David, can you smile for us?" I would always give a weak half smile. The right side of my mouth would move into a faint grin and the left side of my mouth would remain still. My family later told me that they didn't care how many tests I passed, so long as I passed the smile test.

On the Monday evening after the surgery, the doctors took a postsurgery MRI. Unfortunately, this revealed some disheartening news. At some point either during or after the surgery, I had suffered a stroke. And not just any stroke—it was a pretty severe stroke. This was terrible news for my family, and especially for my wife. The doctors explained to them that I would experience a large decrease in mobility and coordination and that I might never be able to walk again. It then made sense to them why I had such a hard time feeling or moving anything on my left side.

That was a tough day for my family. They all sat in my room in the ICU, looking at me, hoping that I would come back and be the dad they had always known. None of them knew what the stroke would do to me. None of them knew what the upcoming months would bring. Many tears had been shed in those few days, and it just didn't seem like they would be stopping any time soon. Considering I had arrived at the hospital in such bad shape, and then had a brain surgery and a stroke, there was no telling how long it would take before I would be back. The doctors counseled my family to be patient and told them it would be a very gradual process. Progress would be measured in weeks, not in days.

Finally, only a few minutes after my family received the news about the stroke, I began to wake up a little. I hardly moved my mouth but was able to get out the word "glasses." My family understood and grabbed my glasses for me. I was in and out of sleep, but I kept saying very slowly, "I want the wet lips." I guess Susan had been giving me kisses and I liked it. Plus, I was so 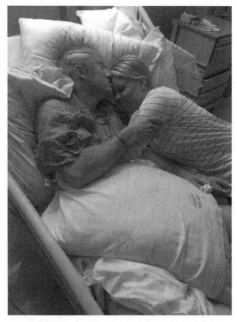 dang thirsty from the sodium they were putting in me through the IV. I desperately wanted a drink, but because they were worried that I would aspirate anything I ate or drank, they had to continue feeding me through the tube. I just remember wanting a drink so bad, and no one would give it to me! But my kids and wife knew that if I was asking for a kiss from my wife, then I was probably the man that they had always known. Those little steps of progress gave them all hope.

I spent six nights in the ICU, with small improvements every day. I began talking/mumbling more and more, but most of what I said involved asking for water. The hospital gives out free drinks to everyone staying there, but my family had to stop bringing in any drinks to the room because I was pestering them for anything. I was asking for Mountain Dew, Diet Coke, and anything you can think of. In fact, one of my brothers-in-law is a dentist, and I asked him to get me a glass of sterile saline. I guess I thought that if I aspirated saline then it wouldn't be so bad. I was obviously desperate.

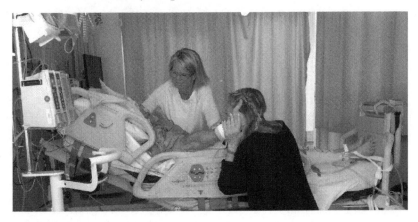

Luckily, the nurses finally let me suck on ice cubes. I still wanted water, but I was content with that compromise because it was better than nothing. Finally, after eight days in the ICU, I was transferred to the rehab floor for those with head or brain injuries. That would become my condo for the next thirty days. It also became the place that helped me relearn to walk and get my life back together.

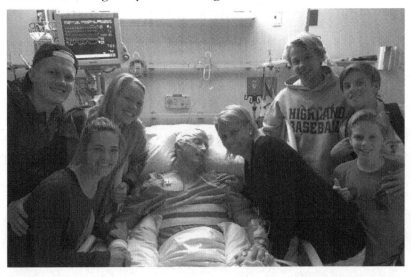

Chapter 9

Adversity's Lessons

The rehab floor is an amazing place. When I was wheeled in from the ICU, I couldn't move my left arm or leg, I couldn't eat without a tube, I couldn't walk or stand, I couldn't use the bathroom by myself, and I was discouraged and frustrated. The rehab team scheduled me for at least one hour of physical therapy, one hour of occupational therapy, and then another thirty minutes to an hour of cognitive therapy each day. Plus, I told all of the trainers that if they had any free time throughout the day, I would love to pick up more therapy time. I think they liked working with patients who wanted to improve, so they were frequently stopping by my room to see if I wanted to do another hour of therapy. It was awesome.

The first week in rehab was somewhat frustrating, because I still had to be fed through the tube running through my nose. And against the doctor's orders, I decided to pull the feeding tube out in the middle of the night, thinking that I was fine to eat on my own. The doctors were upset, told me not to do that again, and put it right back in. Having a giant tube shoved up your nose and down your throat is not a pleasant experience. The pain of putting the tube back in was so awful that I decided to never pull it out again until the doctors told me it was okay to do so.

One of my doctor friends recommended to my children that they bring some family pictures and hang them around the room. He said he always appreciated when his patients' families would do that, because it would show the doctors, nurses, and CNAs that each patient was a real person before this experience. It was easy for the hospital staff to forget that even 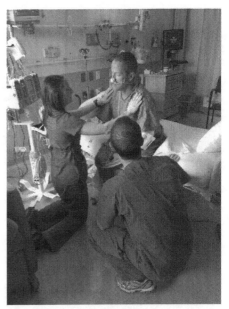 though I needed someone to help me shower, use the bathroom, eat, and stand, I was more than just a helpless patient. My daughter, Sarah, and my daughter-in-law, Karli, liked the idea of decorating, so within a few days, my hospital condo was decorated with several pictures of our family.

I was determined to learn to walk again and wanted to be back at my house as soon as possible. This enthusiasm and determination was important in therapy, but I think it scared my family and the nurses when I wasn't being watched as closely. The head nurse for the floor wrote on my chart that I was "impulsive." In other words, without being able to walk, I would try to get out of bed on my own to use the bathroom or move around. I didn't want to bother anyone, and I felt like I could do it, so I would just try. Luckily, for my own safety and for my family's peace of mind, they set up an alarm on my bed that would go off whenever I tried to climb out.

Losing movement on one side of your body makes you immensely dependent on other people. I knew the theme of becoming more and more dependent would amplify as my life went on, but the first few weeks in rehab, I was the most dependent I had ever been. Showering, using the restroom, walking, and even brushing my teeth required one to two other people there to help. Even if they were more than willing to assist me, I still felt bad always asking for help. Especially because a few weeks prior I was not only able to complete all of these basic tasks on my own, but I was in tip-top shape. I went from riding fifteen miles on a bike every day to needing help with the most basic of tasks. However, it seems like the more dependent I became, the more I realized how lucky I was to have so many people around me willing to help.

Although the shift from my independence to dependence was frustrating at times, I really did appreciate people looking out for me. I cannot express enough how much I love and appreciate the staff at Intermountain Medical Center. The therapists, nurses, CNAs, doctors, and other staff members were so loving and patient with me, yet they also challenged me and helped me learn everything I needed to learn. They would compliment me when I made progress and call me out if I wasn't working as hard as they knew I could. I loved it.

On my first day of therapy, I was instructed to take cones from one pile and put them on another pile. Cone stacking helped me to regain the balance that I lost in the stroke. Stroke patients often lose feeling on one side of their body, which causes the brain to misjudge the center of the body. I would think I was sitting straight, but in fact I was leaning over so much that I was about to fall.

The following weeks of therapy were focused on helping me learn to walk again, improving general coordination, teaching me how to get into a vehicle, and helping me to get coordination back in my hand. Every day we worked harder and tried another exercise. I loved it because I could feel the progress I was making. It was exciting, and I was so grateful to have a team of people who genuinely wanted my success.

As I sat in the hospital, listening to what had happened to me in the prior weeks from my kids and wife, I couldn't believe how close I had been to losing my life. I could feel how much I scared my family, and I didn't like that. But in a way, I felt like this experience was bringing us closer together. Even with one of the captains being a little bit injured, Team

Koelliker was as strong as ever. According to the doctors, I had been "knocking on death's door" and had made it out alive. My family had spent sleepless nights filled with tears, and they had been forced to consider what their lives would be like without me there—and then I came back.

This feeling of barely escaping death, or almost cheating death, gave my family a renewed sense of love and happiness. We were together, and we didn't know how long that would last, so we were determined to live it up and be grateful for whatever time we had. Any time is better than no time, which is what we thought we might have had only a few weeks before.

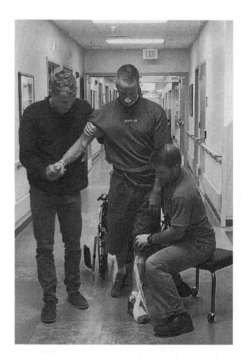

These feelings of love from my family motivated me to work harder during therapy so I could return to being their normal dad as soon as possible. I wanted to be my wife's husband again, not my wife's patient. I stayed determined throughout my time in rehab, working hard, staying focused, and doing everything I could to learn to walk again. After a week I was taking little steps with the therapist, the next week I was walking with the therapist, the next week I was walking with a cane, and the last week I was doing stairs and walking almost everywhere. The progress was liberating, and I couldn't wait to be on my way home. My doctors were always blown away when they stopped by to visit. They knew that I'd just had a serious brain surgery and a massive stroke, and they couldn't believe my progress or trajectory. I had so much to live for, and I wanted to get my life back as much as possible. My family was what gave me motivation to keep going, even when I didn't feel like there was anything left in the tank.

For the first few weeks in the ICU and then on the rehab floor, my family members would take turns sleeping over in my room to make sure I was okay. In the ICU there was only a recliner, but the rehab floor had a small bed in the corner. I loved the company but always felt bad making them stay over. I would get up to use the restroom several times a night, and because I was still very unsteady, they would usually get up to help the CNA and me. However, after about three weeks of my wife

 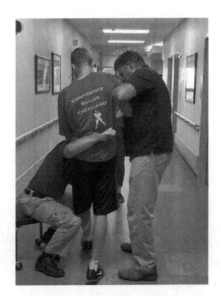

or children sleeping over, we decided that it would be better for them to sleep at home.

The hospital also started allowing me go home for dinner every day to be with Susan and the kids. Then after dinner, someone would drive me back to the hospital, help me get into bed, and wait for me to fall asleep. As soon as the sun would begin to rise in the morning, another family member would be back at the hospital. At this point in time, my two oldest children were in college at Brigham Young University, which was about forty-five minutes away from the hospital. They made that trip up to the hospital almost every day after school. My younger children were busy with school and sports, but they also came over to the hospital almost every day. Consequently, my hospital room was always filled with my immediate family, but there were also so many other people that came out to visit me. My friends, siblings, parents, and children were always at the hospital, supporting me and accompanying me to all of my therapy sessions. I truly am a blessed man.

During one of the nights in the hospital, after the therapy sessions had ended and I had said good night to my family and friends, I found myself lost in thought. It had been a good day, but I couldn't help but face the inevitable truth that I still had a brain tumor. I thought about all the feelings one might have in this situation. In a terminal situation it is so easy to slip into feelings of self-pity, resentment towards others, resentment towards God, anger, or jealousy. But whenever I began to slip into those feelings, I would try my best to cut them off. I wouldn't allow those feelings to cultivate inside of me, because I knew it would only bring me further down.

Death used to be a scary thing for me. Not necessarily because I was nervous for what came after death, but because I had so much to live for. I have an incredible wife whom I love dearly. I have five amazing children, some of whom are still growing up and others who have grown up and found amazing spouses that make our family even better. I want to meet my grandchildren, to be able to play with them and be a loving grandpa and friend to them. I don't necessarily fear death; I just love life.

I've tried to change how I think about death. We are so quick to consider death as the end, but in many ways, I believe death is a new beginning. The beginning of a new chapter. I love a poem by Gordon B. Hinckley called "What Is This Thing Man Calls Death?", which he wrote after his wife passed away. I memorized it after my second surgery, and it has always brought me great comfort. It goes like this:

What is this thing that men call death

This quiet passing in the night?

'Tis not the end but genesis

Of better worlds and greater light.

O God, touch Thou my aching heart

And calm my troubled, haunting fears.

Let hope and faith, transcendent, pure,

Give strength and peace beyond my tears.

There is no death, but only change,

With recompense for vict'ry won.

The gift of Him who loved all men,

The Son of God, the Holy One.

It is such a beautiful poem. I love the lines "Let hope and faith, transcendent, pure,/ Give strength and peace beyond my tears." I've felt my own hope and faith, and the hope and faith of others, lift me out of a pit of despair. The hope that I might be healed, or, more importantly, the hope for a life after this one, has brought peace and happiness to my soul. Whenever it is my time to undergo the "quiet passing in the night," I want my family to know I really believe that I will see them again. This hope and faith makes me feel at peace. "There is no death, but only change." I love that.

I wrote this on my last night in the hospital:

*I am on my 37th night in the IMC hospital, and I go home
tomorrow. It's 11pm and I'm in my room alone. I'm ready to go but
I will miss the wonderful experience I had here with some of the
finest human beings I have ever met. They have inspired me to be
better. To strive harder to look deeper into my soul.*

The following morning, I finished my last rounds of therapy, and in the
afternoon, we prepared to leave the hospital. My siblings and some
friends surprised me in the gathering room next to my room so that they
could celebrate as I walked out of the hospital. There is a tradition the
hospital does for all of their leaving patients. They play the patient's
favorite song while he or she does a loop around the floor, saying
goodbye to everyone on the way out.

Karli, my daughter-in-law, had worked hard to make a mix of a lot of my
favorite songs. After my surprise of seeing all of my family and friends,
we turned on the music and started walking around the hospital floor. I
had my lucky Chicago Cubs cane that one of my best friends had given
me (the Cubs were playing for their first championship in 108 years), and
I was so happy to be leaving the hospital. I started the farewell loop and
waved good bye to the other patients as I passed their rooms.

It was oddly quiet, though, and I wondered where all of my therapists
were. As I looped around the corner to start the final hallway, I saw all of

the therapists, nurses, and CNAs who had helped me lined up on each side of the hall, cheering and clapping while doing wall sits. Walking through their cheers, was one of the best experiences I had ever had. These people had taught me to walk again and had given me hope. We took some pictures and shed some tears, and I gave hugs to everyone. I will never forget that moment.

Chapter 10

Coming Home

It was so great to be home—sleeping in my own bed, hanging out with my children, and just being back in my neighborhood. I loved it. But it didn't take long to realize that I wasn't coming back to the same life. I was still trying to walk without falling, my vision field cut had become significantly worse on the left side, and my left hand had lost almost all of its mobility. Not only could I not drive anymore, but I also couldn't run or bike, either. I felt completely dependent on others, and many times I felt like a burden.

During a conversation with my oldest son, I started to vent about not being able to do the things I loved. I wanted to be able to work, to drive, to ride my bike, and to play sports with my kids. However, after talking with him for a few minutes, we started to identify the underlying reasons for why I enjoyed those activities. After some digging, we started to realize that behind every activity I loved, there was a core feeling, experience, or relationship associated with it. By identifying those core feelings, experiences, or relationships, we started thinking of other ways to reach that same destination.

For example, I always loved playing catch with my sons. But it wasn't really the act of throwing and catching that I loved; what I really loved was being able to spend quality time with my boys, talk about their lives, and feel our relationship being strengthened. Playing catch had just always been the means to accomplish those things, but it wasn't the only way. I learned that I could get the same results by going on walks, sitting on the porch, or enjoying another activity with them that allowed us to spend time together and deepen our relationship.

This discovery also helped me get over the fact that I was unable to work as an endodontist. Even though I really enjoyed my profession, and performing surgeries was fascinating and invigorating, I can't say that I live and breathe root canals. What I truly love about my profession is that I can help people. When someone walked through my office door, I was able to provide a unique service and solve their problem. Although I am no longer able to work as an endodontist, there are still so many ways that I can help others.

Even though I am limited in mobility, and I may get tired a little easier, I still try to find ways to be of value to others. When I find ways to be helpful, even if it's something small, my purpose for living is strengthened. What makes me feel the most tired or depressed, is feeling like my life isn't a help to anyone else. Hopefully, something that I do, maybe even this book, will make the last years of my life mean something.

One of the most meaningful activities that I've been involved in recently is helping with an ice cream shop. On a trip to Newport Beach last year, a close friend of mine, Chris Nielson, told me about an ice cream shop in Dallas, Texas, called Howdy Homemade Ice Cream. Beyond making great ice cream, what makes this business so unique is that that they mainly employ individuals, or "heroes" as they call them, with special needs. It was founded by a good Christian man named Tom with the goal of empowering and uplifting these individuals to accomplish more than what some people might think possible. After hearing this story from Chris, I immediately felt like we needed to bring something like this to Utah. Chris and his wife, Heidi, have a son with special needs, and so this business idea was especially meaningful to them.

Chris and Heidi invited Susan and me down to Dallas with them to learn more about Howdy Homemade. We had such an incredible experience interacting with Tom and the employees, all confirming our feeling that we needed to bring this to Utah. Chris and Heidi have been so kind to include us in this exciting business, but they are the ones who have done all of the heavy lifting. They found a location less than half a mile from both of our houses, bought all of the equipment, and redesigned the entire building. Susan and I would come by often and help when we could, and Chris and Heidi would always stop by our house and give us updates on everything.

We learned to make homemade ice cream and got everything in order for opening day. We met with the local news and did everything we could to spread the word. September 2, 2017, was our grand opening, and we could never have imagined the support we would get from the community. For weeks and weeks there was a line out the door for most of the day. Dozens of incredible special needs individuals are now proud workers at Howdy, and the business seems to be going well. Susan and I don't pretend to take credit for any of this success, but we are so grateful that we've been able to be a small part of this.

As often as possible, I go into Howdy and visit with the many people who come to the shop. I love talking to the customers, and I cherish the relationships I have built with the "heroes" who work there. Since opening, we've developed two main mottos at Howdy: "Every soul matters" and "Come for the ice cream, stay for the people." We want everyone to feel like they are loved, valued, and at home when they visit Howdy Homemade.

Although I don't get the opportunity to work as an endodontist anymore, I have been able to find those same feelings of gratification and success by working and being involved with Howdy. When going through a tough situation like a brain tumor, it is easy to feel like so many doors of opportunity are being slammed shut. However, if we try our best and get a little creative, there are just as many other doors of opportunity that are being opened.

These opportunities are constantly around us, but it seems like this tumor in particular is what has encouraged my family and me to get out and take advantage of the opportunities around us—to enjoy life and say "yes" to doing new things. When you only have a few years left to live, you really don't have time to wait and do something later.

For years, Susan and I had been wanting to take our kids to Europe. Finally, we decided that before our kids started moving out of the house, we needed to make it happen. So this summer we traveled through Switzerland, Germany, Spain, France, and Italy as a family. My four sons, and one newly added son-in-law, would push me around in the wheelchair and lift me up whenever we approached a curb or other obstacle. I know I wasn't the most convenient person to travel with, but I also know we all had a blast. We laughed, ate delicious food, and explored several of the most beautiful parts of the world. It was a trip none of us will ever forget.

Another opportunity that we have tried to take advantage of is working on our family-owned business, Kore Baseball Products. I've always been a big baseball player, and since having kids, batting practice has been one of my favorite activities to do with my sons. On one occasion during batting practice in the summer of 2011, my son hit the cover off of one of the leather baseballs. Instead of throwing the worn leather away, I put it in my pocket and took it home. I stuffed the cover full of cotton, sewed the laces back up, and gave the ball back to my sons. They immediately took it outside to test it out. After about an hour of playing with the ball, they came in with big smiles on their faces, saying that they loved that the ball looked and felt like a real baseball, but was still soft enough to throw at each other without getting hurt.

To make a long story short, I ended up redesigning a few things on that refurbished baseball, creating a logo, and finding a manufacturer to create what we now call the Kore Ball. With the knowledge that I may only have a few more years left to live, I decided that starting a baseball company with my family couldn't wait any longer. I submitted our first big order, and a few months later, we had six thousand Kore Balls dropped off on our front porch.

Everyone in our family got involved with the business, and it grew faster than we could have ever hoped for. We spent countless hours packaging balls, driving to the post office, and shipping all around the United States. We ordered more inventory, and at times we couldn't keep up with the demand for our little baseball. Eventually, we were able to sell in hundreds of toy stores, boutiques, and large-scale department stores across the nation, including Nordstrom and J.Crew. None of us knew what we were doing, but we did it together as a family, and we had a blast while doing it.

These are the types of things that we may never have done if the tumor hadn't put pressure on us to live in the moment. I'm so grateful that we decided to get out and enjoy life, take a few risks, and do fun things as a family.

Another one of the biggest lessons that my family and I learned during my time in the hospital was to live life one day at a time. I know we hear that advice all the time, but when you don't know if you will live one day, five months, or ten years, you really have to live life one day at a time. Every day there is something that can make you happy and something that makes life worth living. I don't know if I would have been very optimistic about this tumor if I'd known at the beginning that I would have seizures, suffer a stroke, undergo three surgeries, stop working, stop driving, not be able to see on the left side, etc. But by just trying to live life one day at a time, I've been able to take this challenge little by little— and be happy while doing it.

Living life one day at a time doesn't mean that every day is a good day. There have been many times when I am walking around the house, around the neighborhood, or up the stairs, and I lose my balance and fall. My body has been beaten up over the last few months, and it will probably continue to take a beating. Luckily, my family, friends, and neighbors are usually close by and can help me get back up. We joke with our neighbors that part of the responsibility of living on our street is to be willing to pull over and pick me up when I've fallen on the sidewalk. We laugh about it, but I've already been helped by several of my neighbors after I've fallen down and can't get back up on my own. The picture to the right is when I went over to let our dog, Manny, out of his little sleeping area and fell right on top of his plastic gate. I just told Susan I was trying to take a nap on Manny's bed.

Since my stroke, I've been trying to be better about laughing and smiling during tough times. My brothers and I call it my "sense of tumor." Instead of complaining about my left hand not working super well, we decided to just nickname my left hand "Carl." Sometimes Carl listens to me and sometimes he doesn't, but Carl always gives us all a good laugh.

My left side frequently surprises those around me, and it even surprises me. I'll be walking slowly, and then all of a sudden my left foot will get caught on something, and I'll tumble to the ground. It's so frustrating, but I try to laugh it off and not let it bother me. So that's what I've decided to do. I might fall a few times throughout the day, but I always try to shake it off and get back up.

Possibly the most frustrating symptom of later-stage brain tumors is urgency or lack of control when needing to use the restroom. There have been several nights when I wake up at 2 or 3 a.m. and walk with my cane to the bathroom as fast as possible, but I just don't make it in time. I then have to clean my room and the bathroom and shower in the middle of the night, which always results in Susan having to wake up and help me. I'm only forty-eight years old, and I'm having problems going to the bathroom. It is so frustrating at times, and it just makes me discouraged. These are some of the things that wear on me and make it difficult to stay positive every day.

It's okay to have rough days, and it's okay to struggle sometimes. But what I want everyone who reads this book to know is that it's also okay to be happy. Serious illnesses, injuries, or trials like this may seem terrible on the surface, but there are so many great things that can come out of them. People are nicer, more selfless, and thoughtful. My friends have become like brothers to me – calling me, texting me, and stopping by to see how I'm doing. A couple of our friends even came to our house to install handicap railings along the stairs and in our restroom. My kids have all stepped up and have done so much to help me. What teenage kid has to help shower their dad or tuck their dad in at night? My wife has made untold sacrifices that continue to amaze me every day. The true goodness of humanity becomes clearer as people step in to lift up someone who is suffering.

Chapter 11

Why Everybody Needs a Brain Tumor

For years, I've been wanting to write this book. Until we started writing, the only thing I knew about the book was that I wanted *Everybody Needs a Brain Tumor* to be the title. However, I knew that if I was going to make such an audacious claim, I'd better be able to explain my reasoning. I felt like sharing my story was the best way to help you understand where I was coming from. I know our writing isn't stellar, but I hope you've been able to look past that and pull something meaningful from these pages.

I still don't know all of the answers to why we must go through such difficult situations in life. In this final chapter, as I talk about why I believe that everybody needs a brain tumor, I invite you to substitute the words "brain tumor" for any difficult challenge you or someone you love has faced. Think of your life's nastiest curveball. I know there are countless amounts of difficult, challenging, and terminal situations people face every single day – many of which are much more difficult than what I've faced. However small, big, trivial, or terminal our personal "brain tumors" might be, they are all unique and can feel insurmountable at times.

As I mentioned earlier in this book, brain tumors kick us out of the driver's seat of life and give us a new life contract. In this contract, we relinquish control of our circumstances, but retain maximum control of who we are and who we will become. Through life's brain tumors we can fully understand and focus on what actually matters. *Understand and focus.* There are times when we may lose control of our lives briefly, and that may bring us perspective for a moment. We might make a bad decision, suffer a small injury, or have a difficult challenge come our way.

Through temporary difficulties, we can begin to *understand* what really matters in life. But as soon as we resolve the issue at hand, we reassume control and forget what we learned. Instead of undergoing the challenging and painful process of personal refinement, we prefer to go back to our old ways with a few life lessons in our back pocket. Malignant brain tumors, on the other hand, permanently knock us out of control. We can't ever go back to life before our diagnosis. This means that we have the opportunity to perpetually *focus* on what really matters in life – on who we are and who we will become for the rest of our lives.

Let me repeat something: these lessons are not just unique to brain tumors. An addiction to drugs, a handicapped child, or any other persistent trial or challenge may teach us the same lessons. And in reality, we all face ongoing difficulties and challenges, big and small, that can help us to understand and focus on what matters most in life. By constantly facing a drug addiction, one is compelled to consider many of life's most challenging questions and must also embark on a never-ending journey of personal refinement. We all qualify to learn these life lessons; however, depending on the seriousness of our trial, it may take more persistence and humility to recognize the learning opportunity.

Viktor Frankl, an Austrian neurologist, psychiatrist, and Holocaust survivor, talks about this concept in his book *A Man's Search for Meaning*. He teaches, "When we are no longer able to change a situation, we are challenged to change ourselves." He continues, "Everything can be taken from a man but one thing: the last of the human freedoms—to choose one's attitude in any given set of circumstances, to choose one's own way." What an amazing lesson from someone who witnessed and underwent an incomprehensible amount of pain and suffering.

By knocking us out of control, brain tumors strip us down to the core. They force us to remove ourselves from behind our personal facade. We are no longer invincible. We become vulnerable. As you know, my brain tumor slowly stripped me of almost everything I was able to do. I can no longer work, bike, drive a car, or walk without help. I even need help using the restroom. My armor and tough-guy facade has been broken down and torn off. The only thing in my control is the core and essence of who I am.

Initially, I think it is natural for all of us to grasp for anything we can get our hands on and try to control our situation. In my fight against cancer, I've tried multiple surgeries, countless types of therapy, and various chemotherapy treatments and other medications. It is not bad to get out and fight for anything you possibly can. However, what made this tumor so powerful and transformational is that even though I am constantly trying to get back on my feet, I've decided to not base my happiness on what ultimately happens with my health. In other words, my happiness is rooted in things that I can always control: my character, my heart, and my love towards other people.

I'm reminded of some advice I was given long ago: "One only gains control by relinquishing it." I focus on things in my absolute control, and I leave everything else up to God. I submit my will to Him and His plan for me. In many ways, this situation is similar to marriage. In marriage, it's so easy to want your way and do anything you can to get it. However, as you (and hopefully your spouse, too) begin to listen, to accept, and to submit, your relationship grows, and you both become happier. You start to understand each other, to grow closer and to progress. Likewise, this process of submission to God teaches us to understand His will a little better, to grow closer to Him, and to progress.

The principle of forgetting about what you want, or submitting your will, is not a new concept. In fact, it is almost two thousand years old. Christ taught in Matthew 16:25, "For whosoever will save his life shall lose it: and whosoever will lose his life for my sake shall find it." If you try to control or save your life, you will lose it. If you lose or submit your life to God's will, you will find it. If you can afford to let go of everything you want to control in your life, you start to focus on what really matters, and you find what life is all about.

This is a difficult and frightening process, because it makes you vulnerable. In many ways, you feel exposed. I felt as if the strong and capable guy I once was had been de-masked and uncovered. But is that a bad thing? I always thought being vulnerable meant being weak. But that isn't it at all. Being vulnerable and exposed helps you be your authentic, true, and imperfect self. It reveals the core of who you are. And interestingly enough, being vulnerable helps others to be their authentic, true, and imperfect selves as well.

This vulnerability has literally changed the nature of my relationships. Instead of my relationships being built on a foundation of respect, my relationships are now based on love. Being vulnerable helps those around me feel like they can be vulnerable too. I mean, would you feel the need to be super impressive while hanging out with a guy who doesn't work, can't ride a bike, can't drive, is blind on his left side, and is just trying to make it to the bathroom in time? I hope not.

Whenever I go to lunch with a friend or family member, we may talk briefly about work or whatever is going on in our lives, but we most often focus on the good stuff. We talk about our kids, good memories, the meaning of life, and how to live one day at a time. We talk about our fears, our worries, and our weaknesses. Can you imagine trying to gossip about someone in front of a guy like me? Or even worse, can you imagine a guy like me trying to gossip about someone else? I'd have to really stretch to come up with anything, because at this point you guys probably do most things better than me anyway. Gossiping, for me, is a dead end every time.

My brain tumor has accelerated my ability to be vulnerable, and by so doing, it has accelerated the deepening of my relationships. However, it doesn't take a brain tumor for us to be vulnerable with each other. Being vulnerable doesn't have to be about sharing your deepest, darkest secrets. I think sharing challenges is part of it, but it mostly seems to be about being genuine, not having ulterior motives or selfish designs. Opening up to others and being vulnerable shouldn't be selfish or focused on yourself. It is an acknowledgement of your weaknesses, coupled with a genuine care for others. By acknowledging your own weaknesses and challenges, you make others feel comfortable in doing the same.

So what is the path like from diagnosis to peace? And is there even a path? Well, to start out, I feel very strongly that there is a path. But each person has a unique path. Without any doubt in my mind, that first night and week after I was diagnosed with a brain tumor were the worst of my life. The pain and anguish were almost too much to bear. Eight years later, I am not cured. In fact, I am much worse from a medical perspective than I have ever been. However, I am also in a much better place from a happiness perspective than I've ever been in the past eight years.

When I was a young endodontist studying at Temple University, it was ingrained in us as students that we were not trying to take away our patients' pain. Rather, we were trying to create an environment where they could heal. Healing relieves pain. We are the architects of the healing environment, but we don't do the healing ourselves. Likewise, since my diagnosis I have tried to foster an environment of healing for myself—an environment that helps me move towards peace and happiness. I can't lift the pain and tumor out of my body, but I can allow this vulnerability and this challenge to heal me in other ways. I can be perfected and made whole through this challenge.

I especially don't want it to seem like I think I'm better than others because I was diagnosed with a brain tumor. That is ridiculous. Many people go through much more challenging circumstances every day and don't have the same support that I have had. However, whatever issues you have faced, big or small, these lessons are applicable. For me, it took a literal brain tumor to teach me some of these lessons. For you, it might not take as much. So how can we all apply these lessons right now, without waiting for a tumor to come our way?

I think it begins with spending less time and energy focused on changing our circumstances and more on changing who we are as individuals. We need to focus on the core of who we are, on our character, our personality, our patience, our love, and our true selves. One of the best ways to start doing that is to not be afraid to be vulnerable. Share your worries, your concerns, and your insecurities with others. Ask people for help and advice. Don't be afraid to uncover and expose more of who you are.

We seem to do everything within our power to get others to love and respect us. Yet the way we approach that is to get them to think we are smart, talented, or gifted in some unique way. In reality, the people we develop the deepest relationships with are usually people who feel comfortable sharing their vulnerabilities. It is part of the reason why people love newborn babies. Yes, babies are adorable, but they are also vulnerable and need us to survive. So mothers, fathers, and others step up and do things they would never consider doing for someone otherwise. This results in a powerful bond of love between the parent and the child.

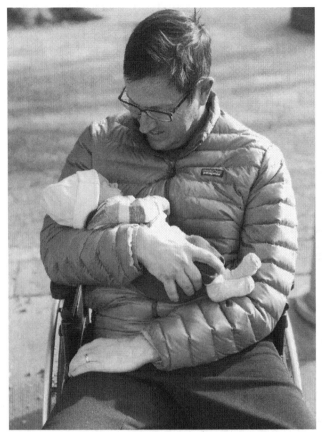

Me with my grandson, Cal

On the other side of the vulnerability coin is the importance of listening to others and their vulnerabilities. I think we all can be better at listening to other people's worries, concerns, and frustrations. Not so we can fix them, but so people can feel loved and understood. When we listen to others and try to understand their challenges and vulnerabilities, our relationships deepen. We become softer with others. More thoughtful and more patient. People are already like that with me. I move so slow and can be such an inconvenience, but my friends and family don't treat me like that. They know I have a brain tumor, so they are more loving and more patient. I think if we all listened to each other a little more and tried to understand each other's "brain tumors," we would all be a little more loving and kind.

The final recommendation I have is to think about the "why" that drives your life. Why do you wake up every day? Why do you work hard to support or raise your family? If you were to be stripped of everything you used to be able to do, why would you still get out of bed in the morning? Everyone's "why" may be different, but understanding and focusing on that "why" can give us direction and peace.

I wanted to share with you my "why," or, in other words, my reasons for wanting to live when there are so many things that seem to be wanting me to die.

I want to live because I love life. Specifically, I love the people in my life. I want to live for them. My relationships with friends and family have literally kept me alive through this experience. The bonds of love that connect us have given me the will and the means to live. I always had good friends and a great family, but only through this experience have I realized how blessed I really am.

My friends come over often—some to help me with my therapy, some to go on walks, and others just to catch up and talk about life. My siblings come over to my house all the time to drive me to the store, exercise with me, and make sure I am doing okay. My kids help me get dressed and escort me as I walk around the house, and they are always right by my side. My incredible wife makes sure I'm always taken care of, tucks me in at night, and gets up with me in the middle of the night when I need something. I truly believe that no one will know Susan's real greatness except for me. I can't even begin to describe everything she has done and the burden she has chosen to shoulder for all of us. She is incredible.

The other day I wrote this in my journal:

> *As I think about this book, there are some very core beliefs that I want to share that seem to have been solidified through this experience. First is my belief in a loving God. One who looks out for us, who knows our individual worries and concerns. The second is the eternal nature of relationships. I truly believe that families and friends can be together after this life. That belief and hope has sustained me.*

Without any doubts in my mind, the most important thing I have learned through this experience is the power of love. When I had just started chemotherapy in the spring of 2016, we had a family meeting and decided that our family motto would be "Live with love today." We don't know what tomorrow will bring, and we can't change what we have done in the past, but one thing we do know is that we are capable of loving those around us today. I live with love today, because I live by love every day. I've felt God's pure love countless times throughout this experience, both directly from Him and also through the people around me. It keeps me going and helps me feel like I have purpose in meaning in my life. Love is why I chose to live.

I hope this book has been helpful to you. I'm not the best writer, and I certainly don't have all the answers to life's questions. I also realize that I have been tremendously blessed in more ways than one. I've lived almost eight years with a brain tumor. That's several years past what experts thought I would live. I have friends and acquaintances who didn't get nearly as much time as I did, and many of these people probably learned most of these lessons much quicker than me.

My faith in God and in His plan for me and my family has sustained me throughout this experience. I was always a religious person, but as Joseph Smith (the first leader of the LDS church) said, "I've waded in tribulation lip deep, and it has only brought me that closer to deity." I believe in God and Jesus Christ with my whole heart. I urge you to look to God during difficult times and good times. My relationship with Him has provided peace and hope beyond comprehension. It is my foundation and my rock.

As I mentioned in the preface, our understanding of life deepens as we experience the law of opposition in all things. We appreciate the light because we've experienced the dark. We appreciate the sweet because we've tasted the bitter. Even though life can be so incredibly difficult at times, it is in those challenging moments when we start to appreciate and understand how truly sweet it is to be alive.

If nothing else, I hope the message is clear that, although challenging beyond belief, brain tumors and other trials can actually enrich and bless your life. On the surface, these things seem terrible and are difficult to swallow. But as we dig deep within ourselves, we discover a depth to our relationships and a more profound love that enriches our lives and the lives of those around us.

May we think of tough times as opportunities: Opportunities to learn. Opportunities to serve. Opportunities to bring our world a little closer together. Some people look at my situation and think, "Wow, that poor man. He has been battling a brain tumor for eight years." Yes, I've experienced some things that have been discouraging, but I still have so much to be grateful for. Every morning and night I get on my knees and thank God that I've been given just one more day. Every day is a huge opportunity. This brain tumor is an opportunity. An opportunity to live life as it ought to be lived.

And, as hard as it may be, I am grateful for that opportunity.

A Final Note from David's Son

Writing this book with my dad was an amazing experience, but watching him live through the stories in this book was truly miraculous. He has wanted to write this book for years, but he never had the time or felt the urgency to actually write it. However, after his recent stroke and third surgery in the fall of 2016, we were sitting in the hospital together, and I felt like we needed to make it happen. This experience has taught him so much, and I, for one, did not want those lessons to go unshared. Beyond the lessons he's learned, my dad has literally become a different person. He's always been a great guy, but this experience has refined and molded him into a much better version of himself. It has made him quicker to forgive and slower to become angry. It has humbled him and made him the most loving person I know. The true miracle of my dad's fight with cancer is the person he has become.

For those of you who know my dad, I'm sure you've had your own personal and unique experiences with him that have brought you two together. My dad is a relationships guy. He doesn't care who you are, what you look like, or what you've done, he is your friend. As you know, my dad was an endodontist by profession, and even though I actually think he found enjoyment in doing root canals (weird, I know), his favorite part of being an endodontist was having the opportunity to develop relationships with his patients. We can hardly go out to eat as a family without one of his patients coming up to us and telling us how much they like our dad. I don't know about you, but if I were to see my dentist in public, I probably wouldn't be going over to say hello. Most of us don't love the person giving us a root canal, and we probably don't expect them to love us, but my dad's patients are different.

It reminds me of an experience I had with him in the spring of 2016, around the same time he was starting chemotherapy and radiation. My dad was invited by one of his patients to speak at the Veterans Affairs hospital church service. This patient had apparently become a close friend of my dad's, as they had enjoyed long conversations about life in the dental chair. My dad invited a few of us to come along with him, so we hopped in the car and headed up to the service on a Sunday morning.

Before my dad got up to speak, his patient, who was conducting the service, stood up to give an intro on my dad. What he said will stick with me forever:

"Well, brothers and sisters, we are privileged to hear from Dr. David Koelliker today. As you know, when we have guest speakers come to our church service, I like to give a bio on the speaker so you know what our guest does for a living and a few of their accomplishments. But when I asked David to send me over a bio that I could use for his introduction, he said, 'Oh, just tell them all that I am your friend.' So here is David Koelliker, my good friend."

I'm not sure if that meant anything to anyone else in that congregation, but it meant everything to me. Above anything that my dad has accomplished in his life, he wants to be known as a friend. That's the kind of guy he is. He is friends with everyone—the troubled high school kids, the homeless woman downtown, and our cleaning lady's son, who has been in and out of rehab. He helps, he listens; he is there when you need him and when you don't. He is the definition of a genuine friend.

This story also speaks to the humility that my dad has always shown. I always thought it was funny that in an attempt to teach me and my three brothers how to work, my dad ended up trimming or mowing neighbors' lawns with us for several hours almost every Saturday when the weather was good. He obviously didn't need or take any of the money we kids earned, but he wanted us to both learn how to work and know that we are never too good for a little manual labor. He didn't think it was weird to be mowing all of his neighbors' lawns; he was with his boys, and he was making sure we didn't feel spoiled or entitled.

There are so many qualities that I admire in my dad, all of which have been accentuated through his fight with his tumor. I've mentioned his love, his friendship, his kindness, and his hard work. The last crowning quality about my dad that I will share with you is his loyalty. My dad is a fiercely loyal person in all aspects of his life. He is loyal to his beliefs, loyal to his friends, loyal to his kids, and loyal to his wife. The kids always joke that if we got kidnapped and taken to the top of the highest peak in Utah, my mom would try to save us by negotiating masterfully with the kidnappers, and my dad would take off running up the mountain and would not stop until he saved us. I don't want this quality to be mistaken for blind loyalty, because it is not. My dad's loyalty is a type of unbreakable determination and faithfulness to protect, defend, and help anyone and anything that he loves and believes in. It is a noble and God-like quality, and it's something that comes as a given in all of his relationships.

It has been hard to watch my dad's health decline since his stroke and third surgery, but it has also been incredible to see how he has responded to each new challenge. He is always happy and pleasant, even with so many things to complain about or be upset about. His tumor has affected his organizational skills and his ability to keep track of time, and he sometimes struggles to remember things that happened only a few hours previously. However, the core of who he is and what he values is still very much intact. He loves God and is as devoted and faithful as ever.

In fact, even while hardly being able to walk, he still always tries to get on his knees to say his prayers. Sometimes, it takes two or three of us to get him up after he finishes praying. One evening, when only he and my mom were home, she had to call some of my dad's friends to come help her get him off the ground after he finished praying. His example has stuck with me whenever I think I'm too tired or too busy to kneel down and pray.

My dad's love for his friends and his family has also stayed with him even as his health declines. He loves his friends. He works out, goes on walks, goes to the temple, goes out to lunch, and does just about anything he can with his friends. He tells me all the time how much he loves his friends and how lucky he feels to have such good people in his life looking out for him. It is true. I've seen all of the amazing people who have gone out of their way to help him out. You know who you are, but you probably will never know how much it really means to my dad.

My dad's love for his family continues to bring us all closer together during this tough time. He has become increasingly dependent on us, but he continues to be a leader of Team Koelliker. His love keeps us going and has strengthened all of us, especially my mom, to keep going, even when times get especially difficult. My mom has been an absolute warrior throughout this experience. I can't even begin to cover the sacrifices that she has made to keep this family going. She is such an incredible woman.

A few weeks ago, as I was helping my dad find something on his phone,

I stumbled on a list that he had quickly typed out. I wanted to share it with you.

Places you'll find my spirit when I die:

-The temple

-Playing catch with your kids

-Helping other people

-Smiling at someone who is having a down day

-Scipio, UT

-Howdy

What a great list. I know when my dad is gone, I'll always be able to feel his presence by doing something or going somewhere on that list. I encourage you to do the same.

One of my favorite proverbs that my dad always shared with us was "Thee lift me, and I'll lift thee, and we'll ascend together." That is the kind of life he has lived. One of lifting others. And even though we've had to lift him during this past year, he has still lifted us more than we'll ever be able to lift him. I hope that through this book and your memories of him, his legacy will continue to lift all of us for years to come.

I love you, Dad.

75745552R00073

Made in the USA
San Bernardino, CA
04 May 2018